Liberating the Law

Liberating the Law

Creating Popular Justice in Mozambique

Albie Sachs
Gita Honwana Welch

Zed Books
London and New Jersey

Liberating the Law was first published by Zed Books Ltd,
57 Caledonian Road, London N1 9BU, UK and 171 First Avenue,
Atlantic Highlands, New Jersey 07716, USA, in 1990.

Cover designed by Andrew Corbett.

Typeset by EMS Photosetters, Thorpe Bay, Essex
Printed and bound in the United Kingdom
at Biddles Ltd, Guildford and King's Lynn.

British Library Cataloguing in Publication Data

Sachs, Albie, *1935–*
Liberating the law : creating popular justice in Mozambique.
1. Mozambique. Criminal law. Justice. Administration, history.
I. Title II. Welch, Gita Honwana
364.679

ISBN 0-86232-920-5
ISBN 0-86232-921-3 pbk

Library of Congress Cataloging-in-Publication Data

Sachs, Albie, 1935–
Liberating the law : creating popular justice in Mozambique / Albie Sachs, Gita Honwana Welch.
p. cm.
Includes index.
ISBN 0-86232-920-5 ISBN 0-86232-921-3 (pbk.)
1. Law – Mozambique – History and criticism.
2. Justice, Administration of – Mozambique – History.
I. Welch, Gita Honwana. II. Title.
LAW
349-679–dc20
[346.79] 90-39968
CIP

Contents

Introduction 1

1. **Liberating the Land, Liberating the Law** 27
   Introduction 27
   The Official Explanatory Note to the Mozambican Land Law: An Overview 28
   The Purpose: What was the Land Law Intended to Achieve? 31
   The Land Law and Revolution 37
   Conclusions 44
2. **The Question of Access to the Courts** 46
3. **Changing the Terms of the Debate: A Visit to a Popular Tribunal in Mozambique** 55
   The Evolution of Popular Justice 58
   The Problem of a Unitary Legal System 60
4. **Transforming Family Law: New Directions in Mozambique** 64
   Introduction 64
   The Diversity of the Mozambican Family 66
   A Unified Legal System 70
   Appendix A: Extracts from the Basic Record of a Local People's Tribunal 76
   Appendix B: Justice that Kills in order to Spread the Faith and Empire 78
5. **The Bride Price, Revolution, and the Liberation of Women** 86
   Introduction 86
   The Various Dimensions of *Lobolo* 89
   Lobolo Today in Mozambique 92
   Lobolo and the Liberation of Women 93
   The Legal Status of *Lobolo* Today 97
   Cases Heard in Community Courts at the Local Level 100
   The Family Law Project 101
   The Extraordinary Conference of the Organization of Mozambican Women 104
   Conclusion 106

6. **The Two Dimensions of Socialist Legality: Recent Experience in Mozambique** 111

7. **Beyond Pluralism: The Mozambican Experience** 124

The Dualist Legal System of Colonial Times 126

Unity, the Central Theme in the Struggle for National Liberation 127

Ethnic-Cultural Diversity and Legal Unity 129

Index 133

Introduction

The problem was not so much how to define the new legal system, as how to implement the changes that were necessary to bring it into being. The theory was clear: completely dismantle the colonial state apparatus and replace it with a new one designed to serve the interests of the mass of the people. Unlike other newly independent African states, where the emphasis had been on continuity and the least possible disruption, Mozambique sought to scrap completely the whole state apparatus inherited from the years of colonial domination and replace it with a totally new one. It is important to stress that this was not simply an ideological option. Independence had been won after ten years of bitter warfare, and when negotiations finally took place between Frelimo and the Portuguese authorities, the subject of the negotiations was the transfer of power and not the terms of independence. Thus, the constitution of Mozambique was not the product of any negotiations but rather a document produced by the Central Committee of Frelimo. Even more important was the fact that, during the armed struggle, large zones of northern Mozambique had been cleared of the colonial presence, and the embryo of a new state was already being established there. These areas, called liberated zones, were seen as alternative areas to the colonially dominated portions of Mozambique, producing different structures of government and run according to completely different principles. The practical problem, therefore, at the time of independence was how to transfer to the whole of Mozambique the institutions, styles of work, attitudes and principles that had already been operative in the liberated zones.

This means that a number of policies adopted elsewhere in Africa were rejected in Mozambique. Thus the policy of Africanization was seen as doubly wrong. In the first place it had a racial or racist connotation that was unacceptable in that it implied that only blacks should be given positions of leadership in the new society. But more important than that, the concept of Africanization presupposed the taking over of the existing colonial state apparatus and simply substituting local Africans for foreign Portuguese within it. In other words, the state apparatus could remain the same and the only difference would be change in the colour of the skin. As Samora Machel once put it, 'some people don't mind being eaten by a local lion as long as they're not devoured by a foreign tiger'. Similarly, the concept of African socialism was looked at rather critically. The Mozambican leaders rejected the idea of a continental socialism that was somehow separated from the struggles of peoples for independence, for development and for social reconstruction throughout the world. Equally, the paternalistic idea of socialism for Africa, that is, a socialism developed in one part of the world and exported to Africa was also scorned. Thus, as one Mozambican leader put it, the idea was unacceptable that seeds were being taken from one part of the world and planted in another to produce similar trees there; the correct approach was that the struggles of the peoples of the world constituted one giant tree, a single tree, but fed by many roots.

In order to understand the specific features of the post-colonial state, it is necessary first to examine the specific features of the colonial state that was being replaced. The legal system in colonial times in Mozambique had three principal characteristics: it was fascist, it was colonial and it was elitist or class-dominated. To say it was fascist is not simply to apply a term of abuse. Portugal for forty years was under a dictatorship in which many of the features of the earlier liberal society had been crushed. In Portugal itself, that is, in the metropole, it was not possible to get a fair trial in a political case. The PIDE (the Portuguese secret police) dominated directly or indirectly all legal decisions; they developed a sophisticated form of torture and interrogation and designed means to prevent accused persons from having open trials or from being properly defended. Thus in Mozambique, a colony of a dictatorship, the small space that had existed in British colonies or in apartheid South Africa for using the courts as a platform for exposing the nature of colonial or racist domination, or for exposing abuses by interrogators, or for putting forward demands of the oppressed people, simply did not exist. Whereas in British colonies the legitimacy of domination was projected through concepts of legality, in the Portuguese colonies it was done first through concepts of Christian trusteeship, and then of multi-racialism and Luso-tropicalism.

In addition to being fascist, Portugal was underdeveloped. This meant that Mozambique was the colony of an underdeveloped dictatorship, unable to compete with its economically more powerful neighbours. Thus the colonial state was used far more directly to control labour in Mozambique than was the case in the neighbouring countries where economic forces played a large role. Forced labour in relation to public projects was common, with heavy taxes imposed on the rural population to force them to leave their lands and work for the colonial state or on plantations or for other private employers. Likewise, forced cultivation, especially of cotton, was widely imposed. The *palmatoria*, i.e., a punishment delivered by means of a beating on the hands, became the symbol of the colonial legal system. The courts were hardly used at all, the domination was direct. This had another important consequence in that the chiefs were heavily and directly involved in the system of domination in the rural areas. Independent chiefs had long been stripped of their authority, many of them being deported to the prison island of Ibo, from which few returned. On the whole, the chiefs were minor subalterns in the colonial apparatus. When colonialism fell, the system of the chiefs fell with it, with significant consequences for the new legal system.

The second characteristic of the legal system in colonial times was, of course, that it was colonial. It was completely dominated by Portuguese laws, Portuguese legal officers and Portuguese legal thinking. All the legislation was made in Portugal and then applied to the colony. As one commentator put it, the laws were shipped out to Mozambique like wine or wool. It was not only the laws that came from Lisbon but the lawyers. All the judges and prosecutors belonged to the Portuguese state service, and the legal profession consisted almost entirely of Portuguese persons who had gone out to the colony to make their fortunes. No law school existed in Mozambique until the very eve of independence and the handful of Mozambicans who were able to think of becoming lawyers and who had the qualifications and moral courage to do so, had to bear the expense of going to Portugal for years of study. All decisions concerning the operation of the law in Mozambique, however great or however tiny, were ultimately taken in Lisbon. The Portuguese legal codes were applied in Mozambique as they were applied in Portugal, even though the social system and cultural values were totally different.

Third, the colonial legal system was strongly designed to serve the interests of the wealthier rather than the poorer sections of the colonists themselves, that is, those who controlled the banks, insurance companies and the large plantations. Legal skills and the laws were all oriented towards securing the interests of these sectors of colonial society, whereas the poorer whites received few benefits. Thus, the law was extremely expensive and access to the courts depended very much on the size of one's pocket.

The task facing the builders of the new Mozambican legal system was therefore both clear and daunting. It was to build a system that was neither fascist nor colonial nor elitist. Concretely, it meant establishing a system that was popular, Mozambican and democratic.

And to carry out this task, there were about two dozen law students about to set off in brigades to establish a whole new legal system, included amongst them one of the authors of this book. And sitting in the audience listening to the special preparatory lectures that were being given to the students, was the other.

This book deals with the first decade of experience in building a new legal system on new principles in Mozambique. Gita Honwana Welch was one of the young judges who worked in the provinces to establish the legal system. Albie Sachs was in the early years of his eleven-year stay in the country, a law professor at the University of Eduardo Mondlane, where he taught international law and family law. Later Gita was appointed Head of the Department of Research and Legislation in the Ministry of Justice, and when the Law Faculty was closed down (in circumstances referred to in the essay on socialist legality), Albie came to join her as Director of Research. This book consists essentially of papers produced over the years to explain the evolution of the Mozambican legal system, and especially its 'popular' character, to international audiences. The actual establishment of the new court system is not directly referred to in the essays. What happened was that the law students were sent out by the Ministry of Justice to establish a series of pilot schemes as the basis of the new court system in Mozambique. Two students went to each province, acting as judges and prosecutors, where, over a period of time, and on the basis of meetings with the local population, they established what were called popular tribunals in a number of localities and districts, as well as ensuring the functioning of a Provincial Court. The students were required to write up their experiences in the form of a diary/report which was then sent every fortnight to the ministry in Maputo. On the basis of the preliminary experiences of these brigades in the provinces, a generalized pilot scheme was established to be applied throughout the whole country on an equal basis. This scheme was worked out at a meeting in Maputo in which all the members of the brigades took part, together with personnel from the Ministry of Justice and others directly interested in the subject.

The generalized pilot scheme was put into operation for about nine months, and on the basis of the new experience gained, a meeting was called under the title of the First National Conference of Justice. A large commission at that conference was given the task of drafting the basis of a new Courts Act for Mozambique, and in this way the legal foundation of the new court system was established. The draft of the new legislation and the court system was then widely circulated throughout Mozambique and, in the light of observations made, certain amendments were introduced. The result was that eventually the national Popular Assembly adopted the *Law on Judicial Organization* in 1978 in terms of which a hierarchy of courts was established, starting with purely elected popular tribunals at the level of the base, proceeding to district courts and thereafter to provincial courts, with the objective of creating a Supreme Court as the final court of appeal and the court that would supervise the whole judicial structure. At the time of writing this Introduction (1989), the Supreme Court had been created and the first generation of Supreme Court judges, comprised of veterans of the justice brigades of 1978 but now with a decade of rich and difficult experience behind them, appointed. The court structure is complete and, at least in institutional terms, the basic aims of the Law on Judicial Organization have been achieved.

The essays in this book do not deal specifically with the court structure. Rather, they concentrate on the basic principles which guided the courts in their operation as well as the difficulties encountered. It was not always easy to communicate to international audiences the experiences gained in Mozambique. In some cases we had to explain that Mozambique was on the south-east coast of Africa, that it had been a Portuguese colony for 500 years, that it had gained its independence after ten years of armed struggle, and that only in 1975, with virtually no personnel or resources, had it started to build a new legal system. But the problems of explanation were more fundamental than simply those of location in geography and history. Like all original experiences, Mozambican experience just did not fit in. We had to face immense theoretical incredulity. There were those scholars who, whenever they heard the term 'popular' or 'people's' applied to any institution, immediately reached for their liberal smelling-salts. It was impossible for them to believe that a people's court could actually be a highly democratic institution, extremely sensitive to local opinions and aspirations, and flexible in its operation. The contrary view of a people's court as a type of programmed or kangaroo court was so strong in their heads that we frequently found it advisable in trying to convey the real and experienced (and in our view, highly interesting) reality in Mozambique, not to use the term people's court, but rather to refer to 'community courts'; 'popular' is bad, but 'community' is good. Once the good description was applied, the way was open for a proper hearing.

Another difficulty encountered was in relation to persons who positively liked the idea of people's courts, who, when they heard the phrase 'rule of law', reached for their revolutionary smelling salts. In this case, the tendency was to give positive marks to Mozambique to the extent that it copied or produced identical replicas of legal forms and ideas to those found in other revolutionary societies. When we pointed out that Mozambican experience drew heavily on aspects of traditional African society, as transformed in the liberated zones, such persons were usually quite disconcerted; they could never grasp what we considered to be the distinction between universality and identity of revolutionary processes.

Another form of intellectual resistance came from Africanist scholars, many of whom we admired very much, who had very fixed ideas about the relationship between what they called imposed law and indigenous law. The whole Mozambican experience went counter to many of their notions, particularly their characterization of the choice facing post-colonial African societies as being that between adopting European-derived, urban-based and elite-oriented ('imposed') law, on the one hand, and traditional, rural and mass-based law on the other. The popular justice or community-oriented system in Mozambique was in fact derived from the experience of the organized peasantry in the liberated zones, extended and adapted to the towns. Instead of presupposing a dualism between a single state law for the elite and a multiplicity of local customs and usages for the masses, it was founded on the principle of a single, constitutionally-based and democratically-operated law for the whole society 'from the Rovuma to the Maputo', i.e., from north to south. It was both indigenous and anti-traditional at the same time, being based on the democratic aspects of African tradition but transforming them and rejecting the feudal and divisive aspects. In Samora Machel's vivid phrase, 'for the nation to live, the tribe must die'.

We had much to be grateful for to the Africanist scholars, however. Their scepticism forced us to sharpen our arguments. It was not enough to know as a fact that illiterate or barely literate peasants were week in and week out carrying on activities that pro-African scholars in Europe and North America had proved to be impossible; we had to start to theorize the experience and enter the debate at a scientific rather than a purely anecdotal ('we were there') level. At times we felt like the new explorers of Africa recounting to learned societies in Europe the marvels we had encountered deep in the African countryside. More fundamentally, the Africanist scholars reminded us that to kill tribalism is one thing, to kill the language and the multiple cultural customs associated with the tribe is another. If, as Samora pointed out, the nation was not just a collection of tribes and races living in a common country with a common flag, if, as he emphasized, the nation was present in every factory, farm, village, school, hospital and court, it was also true that the local languages, customs and ways of doing things were present in the nation (a theme that Samora stressed in the later years of his life).

Finally, we had to deal with what can only be called third world romanticism, in terms of which all the hard and sharp questions of the Third World are subsumed into a kind of vague, populist, developmentalist approach, which is hardly useful in solving the very acute problems which the Third World faces. We were naturally proud to contribute our experience in a third world country towards enriching the debate on the questions of development and transformations, and it is thus appropriate that the book starts with the essay that contains a certain degree of romanticism.

We have left the papers in the original form in which they were prepared, because we feel that the very tone and spirit of the papers in each case conveys useful information, mainly the kind of language being used at a particular moment, and the spirit which was the dominant one amongst those engaged in the project. Readers thus will easily be able to distinguish the rather elated tone of the paper 'Liberating the Land, Liberating the Law' from the doubts and hesitancies in the later paper dealing with socialist legality. If notes of triumphalism exist in this opening paper on the land, we feel that this is not entirely inappropriate. There are moments of triumph as there are moments of defeat in any process of transformation. The triumphalism in that sense was real and the energy which it gave to those who were participating in the process was a major force for change in itself. What is important is not to eliminate triumphalism altogether, but to ensure that it relates only to the real moments of triumph, and never becomes institutionalized or automatic or divorced from its real base. The inevitable consequence of too much triumphalism is too much defeatism. Mozambique has passed through extremely difficult years, assailed by powerful neighbours. It has committed many mistakes, and we certainly participated in those mistakes. The objectives of this introduction then are not only to prepare the reader for the essays that follow, but also to apply a retrospective gloss of analysis to the papers that we wrote over the years.

The transformation of relations on the land constitutes possibly the greatest achievement of the Mozambican revolution. It also constitutes the area of change that is most incomplete, and most full of contradictions. The essay presented here was actually prepared as an introduction for an unofficial translation of the text of the law itself. The introduction and text were published together by the Institute of African Studies at Harvard University around 1980 and subsequently the introduction, with a portion of the text, was modified in a small way, to make it suitable for inclusion in a book entitled *Third World Jurisprudence*. We might mention that the article 'Liberating the Land, Liberating the Law' sat uneasily in that book between texts far less related to radical social transformation and far more relevant to the themes and preoccupations of law schools in essentially Commonwealth countries. The reader will notice that the Mozambican statute dealing with land law is cast in language that is immediately accessible. Accordingly, the introduction was not designed, as introductions to laws normally are, to explain the intricacies of the law, but rather the context in which the law came to be adopted. The open language of the legislation was intended to make the law easily understood by at least the literate population of Mozambique and, indeed, the text was repeated several times over the radio for the sake of those who could not read, or did not have access to the published text.

Here it becomes relevant to say a few words about the relationship between the constitution, legislation and regulations in a society that regards itself as revolutionary. The Constitution of Mozambique, as has already been stated, was not the product of long and intensive debate between lawyers representing the departing colonial power on the one hand, and lawyers representing the emerging new nation on the other. The Constitution was proclaimed by Frelimo on the eve of its greatest victory – the proclamation of independence. By its nature, it had what its authors called a programmatic character. That is, the Constitution not only set out the structure of government and the basic rights individuals, companies, co-operatives or even State economic enterprises declared to be the fundamental themes of the new society, and to provide the broad context in which future developments were to take place. This latter group of themes in their totality constituted a social, political, economic and cultural programme, that had progressively, by means of new legislation, to be materialized. In this sense, a programmatic constitution has a different character from a purely governmental, technical and Bill of Rights type constitution. Thus, the Constitution declared as a basic principle underlining all future legislation in relation to the land, that the land and mineral resources of the country belonged to the State. This basic principle in itself did not indicate how the land was to be used, and precisely how portions of the land were to be identified for particular kinds of use. Nor did it specify what kind of rights individuals, companies, cooperatives or even State economic enterprises could have in relation to the land, nor how these rights were to be protected. Nevertheless, it did indicate as a broad principle that the control of use of the land would not be determined either by feudal domination on the one hand, nor by market forces on the other. It remained for that State, acting through Parliament, to adopt legislation governing all these matters. The land law, therefore, represented one of the most important milestones in the process of materializing the general principles stated in the Constitution.

In order to understand the law better, it is necessary to look to the categories of property contemplated by the Constitution. The Constitution declared that four types of property would be recognized in Mozambique, namely state-owned property, co-operatively-owned property, privately-owned property, and property belonging to the family sector. (Reference to the family sector should be understood as relating to the smallholdings belonging in terms of traditional patterns of ownership or occupation in rural areas to families, and descending from, in terms of the laws or practices of succession, one member of the family to another.) In relation to the land itself, the law contemplated a sector of land belonging to the State in the form of National Parks and other portions to State enterprises; that is, these enterprises would have defined portions of the surface area of Mozambique at their disposal to be used for the purposes of the enterprise. The land law also made provision for the use of land under the control of the co-operative sector, while there are extensive provisions relating to the use of land by the private sector. As the essay indicates, this is the area in which the law played the biggest role because it was the area where the greatest legal, rather than political or administrative, protection of the rights of the land-user were seen to be necessary. Finally, the law referred to and gave protection towards the large portions of Mozambican territory that were being farmed by the family sector on the basis of household production.

Looking back at developments in Mozambique in the decade since the law was adopted, we see that the four basic categories remain intact, but there has been a significant shift in the relative importance attributed to each one of them. At the time the proposed law was being debated, the leadership in Mozambique were confident of a rapid socialization of the countryside. What happened in fact is that the countryside was transformed, not by socialization, but by war. The most dramatic shifts of population and changes in the use of land have to be related to the terrible impact of the destabilization and war inflicted upon Mozambique, which has had catastrophic effects in the rural areas. About one million Mozambicans, out of a total population of 13 million, crossed the borders to receive sanctuary from the war. At least another four million of the rural population became heavily or totally dependent on food aid, because it had become impossible for them to produce the food they needed for their survival and for normal economic activity. The whole of the rural economy was severely disrupted, and infrastructures in the countryside were substantially damaged. It is rather idle to speculate on how rural development and transformation would have taken place in the absence of the war. The war happened and at the time of writing it is still having a pernicious impact. But it seems likely from developments in the economic sector independent of the war, that a substantial amount of rethinking would have been done on patterns of land use, even had it not been for the war.

Thus we might take the Limpopo River Valley as an example. This is an area of land from which African peasants had been forcibly removed in the 1930s and 1940s to make way for peasants from Portugal, settled on smallholdings as a means of establishing the white colonist population and increasing production for the market. The process of expulsion of the people from their traditional lands was one of the factors which induced a patriotic and national spirit in many families in the area, notably that of Samora Machel, whose father was one of the victims of this policy of removal. When independence came and virtually all the settlers in the area abandoned their lands, many of the African peasants felt that they would be able to return to what had traditionally been their landholdings. But the decision was taken to consolidate these small plots into large tracts of land to be operated as state farms, receiving extensive investment and worked by salaried employees. A very large portion of the budget available to the Ministry of Agriculture was allocated to these farms which were intended to constitute the granary of Mozambique. The results in general were disappointing. The vastness of the undertakings and the scantiness of the managerial capacity to run them meant that investment was not properly utilized and resources, which could have been used to stimulate production in other parts of the rural economy, were tied up in an unfruitful way.

Thus in the early 1980s, a process began of adapting the patterns of land ownership and use in the Limpopo River Valley area. The huge conglomerate state-farm sector was broken down into smaller units subject to local decision making and management. Portions of land that had been included in the state sector but were not being utilized were given over, in some cases to co-operatives, but more frequently to a small but growing sector of small- and medium-scale African private farmers. Some of the land was also given back to those families which had traditionally held it. Finally, in the mid-1980s, attempts were made to interest foreign companies in investing in the area. This investment could take place legally in two forms – either by means of a joint venture with a Mozambican enterprise, in terms of which the Mozambican enterprise, frequently a state enterprise, would contribute the land as its share of the initial capital; or by means of an outright leaseholding in relation to productive land. In any event, it became clear that there was considerable competition for the land and that the question of guaranteed title to use of the land had become an urgent one. This was one of the factors which resulted in the publication in 1988 of the regulations governing the implementation of the *Land Act*. It had taken a full ten years to produce this voluminous set of regulations, not only because of the inherent technical problems involved, but because of the evolving situation which required the establishment of appropriate principles for the regulations.

Thus the line of development from the Constitution to the statute of a general kind, and then to regulations of a specific kind is clear. What is required now are the institutions and mechanisms for fully applying the regulations; in particular, the system of registration of title, whether in the urban or in the rural areas, needs extensive reinforcement and expansion.

Another interesting example is that of the co-operatives set up in the Green Belt area around Maputo. Many thousands of persons, about 98 per cent women, work in these co-operatives, which after a very slow and difficult start have succeeded in becoming important sources of production of food for the city as well as centres of independence and dignity for women. To the extent that these co-operatives, by dint of overcoming repeated failures, succeeded in solving problems of transport, marketing, and the planning of production, so they began to insist on increasing autonomy from administrative controls and movement towards a greater degree of guaranteed rights in terms of the law. Thus the co-operative principle does not in any way fly in the face of legality or rule of law; on the contrary, experience in the Green Zones indicates that members of co-operatives can be as insistent on legal rights as any private farmer, and that the definition of boundaries and legal entitlement is not simply a desire of those who wish to put land on the market, but a demand from the co-operative movement itself.

Looking back over the last ten years, we can say that, although in periods of great social upheaval and transformation the question of legal title might at first sight appear to be increasingly irrelevant, in the long run the question has to be faced up to squarely, and appropriate mechanisms have to be created. Similarly, even in a society in which the land is not subject to the principles of the market, and is not a basis for economic transactions in itself, the question of putting an economic valuation on the land does come to the fore. This is not simply because of the competition to acquire the use of fertile, well-watered land, or land accessible to transport; it is a prerequisite for any planning and investment policy, as important to the State and co-operative sectors as it is to the private one. The assumption that the development of the land can take place purely on the basis of social or moral criteria without taking into account economic values at all, or else doing so only in a marginal and perfunctory way, appears to be as false and dangerous to a society which wishes to advance towards socialism as it is to an avowedly capitalist one.

Finally, a word should be said about the important provisions in the *Land Act* relating to ecological questions and to the general topic of the protection of special areas of land. The legislation in this respect was advanced for its times, and bore in mind the relatively large portions of Mozambique which were propitious for nature reserves. Provision was also made for strict control over cutting down or burning of forests and hunting of animals. Mozambique has given a relatively large amount of attention to ecological law. But here again, we see that the war has totally crushed the hopes implicit in the legislation. The nature reserves have been scenes of heavy fighting, and the animals have been slaughtered, in some cases simply for their tusks and in other cases for food. It will be many, many years indeed before the damage can be recuperated.

The question of access to the law cannot be separated from the question of development of the courts and the court structure itself. The article entitled 'Access to the Law in Mozambique' was originally produced as a paper for a conference organized in newly independent Zimbabwe on the theme of access to the law. Its main objective was to show how it was possible to make the courts open to and respected by the citizens even in a country in which very few lawyers existed. In other words, the problem was not simply one of creating more lawyers or establishing legal aid systems, but of altering the procedures of the courts and especially their relationship with the community. Accordingly, we gave great emphasis in the paper to the informality of the system of popular justice and the openness of trials, and what we hoped would be the growing confidence of the community in their system of justice. Looking back over the years that have elapsed since then, we feel, in general terms, more than satisfied with the operation of the popular tribunals, in particular at the grassroots level. We have attended many trials in different areas, frequently coming there unexpectedly, and have been highly impressed by the good relationships that exist between the judges and the community and the general fairness with which the proceedings have been conducted. The tenacity and success of these courts is evident. Whereas at first they took root in the countryside, now they have grown extensively in the *barrios* in the towns. The war has here too had a negative effect but nevertheless, at the time of writing, about 800 of the courts are still in operation. This is an indication that they serve a social function and do so in a way that is acceptable to the community.

The judges are not paid for their work (and we have had no indications that they receive any material reward dishonestly). In fact, in our capacity as research workers undertaking an investigation in relation to the functioning of these tribunals, we have recommended that these courts receive more support, and that, even if the judges continue to act without receiving any emolument, the conditions in which they work be substantially improved. These courts draw heavily on traditions of African justice, in particular on the tradition of extensive popular participation in the resolution of disputes. They generally conduct themselves with considerable patience and dignity and humour, and the absence of lawyers and of the fierce competitive character of a so-called normal trial in no way prevents them from doing basic justice. What is important in relation to their informality is that they do not have the power to send people to prison. In any event, the accused always have the right to appeal. The operation of purely elected popular tribunals at the grassroots level therefore should be seen as one of the great achievements of the processes described in this book. The litigants speak out openly in these courts, they call family, friends, neighbours, workmates to testify on their behalf; the atmosphere is friendly and informal.

It remains to be seen at some future date, when general literacy will have increased, and more infrastructures will have been created, whether the question of the informal procedures of these popular tribunals at the grassroots level will have to be looked at again. In particular, attention will have to be paid to the amount of flexibility and whether local variation is permissible or even desirable in what is regarded as a uniform system of judicial authority. Perhaps it will be necessary to formalize the procedures and to allow for or even require intervention of lawyers in certain cases, perhaps not. What is clear, however, is that the question of training lawyers and the development of the legal profession is one that cannot be left to wait forever.

In Mozambique there can be no doubt that, at the time of independence, lawyers were held in considerable distrust by the general mass of the population. As has been pointed out, the legal system in colonial times allowed virtually no space at all for the defence of either popular or national rights in the courts. The very few lawyers that distinguished themselves by supporting the independence struggle had to act clandestinely; on the surface they were ordinary lawyers making their money by defending those who could afford to pay, but in secret they were giving support to Frelimo and the underground struggle. In addition, a number of law students in Portugal gave up their studies to become full-time militants of Frelimo. There was no body of lawyers known to the general public as defenders of the people's rights, comparable to such as existed in neighbouring South Africa. Experience in other newly independent African countries had not always been too heartening. There, members of the legal profession had often adopted extremely aloof positions, utilizing their skills to amass personal fortunes at the expense of their clients and of the people as a whole. Thus, the decision in Mozambique immediately after independence to abolish private practice in the legal profession and replace it with a system of generalized legal aid, received general public acclaim because it seemed to be a means of ensuring equal access to the courts. Experience since then has shown that, despite the low prestige of the courts and lawyers in colonial times amongst the mass of the people, the question of 'having your own lawyer' is a question that has considerable meaning to the population today, and is one that can only be answered by means of training sufficient lawyers and imbuing them with the necessary skills and courage to fulfil their functions properly. This question and the whole issue of the opening, closing and reopening of the University's Law Faculty will be dealt with at a later stage in this introduction, in connection with the question of socialist legality.

Although not directly referred to in the paper on access to the law, it might be interesting to offer a few reflections on the issue of the evolution of the substance of the law itself in Mozambique. In terms of the principles of popular justice, all legislation was required to have an open and accessible character, in that it could be read and understood by all literate Mozambicans without requiring complicated technical explanations by professionals. By and large this principle has been adhered to, in the sense that virtually all legislation contains a preamble that sets out in a fairly extensive way and in straightforward language the objectives of the legislation and the circumstances which brought it into being. The body of the law itself is then normally expressed in easily understandable language, with a number of useful sub-headings to aid the reader. The fact that these laws, or at least the most important of them, would have been discussed and debated in the Popular Assembly, in which the delegates, mostly of working-class or peasant origin, would have insisted on understanding the terminology they were debating is one reason for the maintenance of this principle. Accordingly, looking at the general body of post-colonial legislation, one can say that the broad principle of open and accessible language has been adhered to, even though certain laws are more technical than others, for example, a law dealing with oil prospecting.

A much greater problem in practice is the fact that a very substantial part of the population does not understand Portuguese, the language of national unity and official communication. In addition, well over half the population is illiterate. Then, even for the Portuguese-speaking, literate section of the population, the problem exists of physically getting hold of the law. Shortages of paper resulting from shortages of foreign exchange have had a disastrous effect on legal publication. Whereas the *Official Bulletins* of the Republic have appeared regularly and thereby established a continuous source of legislation available to subscribers, its reach is necessarily limited. The daily newspapers have normally carried the texts of important new laws, but there have been a vast number of decrees and by-laws which have not been published in the press. The radio has also been a major means of communicating the texts of important new legislation.

One of the problems facing anyone who seeks to find the law on any particular subject is to know whether the law promulgated in colonial times is still in force in that area. The Constitution provided that all legislation in force at the time of independence should continue to remain in force except insofar as it was in conflict with the Constitution or was subsequently revoked by new post-independence legislation. The effect of this provision has varied considerably from one area of the substantive law to the other. Although the essays which constitute this book concentrate more on the guiding principles of the new laws and how they were made operational, rather than on their content, it would not be out of place to mention, in broad terms, which areas have undergone the greatest changes and which have been left relatively untouched.

As a general rule, one might say that public law has been far more affected by post-independence developments than has private law. Thus, obviously, the Constitution itself is totally new and has established new organs of public power and government. The basic territorial divisions of the country underwent relatively minor changes, although there were several substitutions of place names. The army, the police force and the prison corps were totally transformed, in character, personnel and terminology. The civil service was also radically altered, inasmuch as previously it had been a mere extension of the Portuguese civil service. Not only were the existing departments given new functions as part of the new sovereignty and not as mere appendages of colonial administration, but whole new areas were developed and new structures were created. The problem of methods of work, however, was one which had proved far more difficult to change. A colonial style of operation, frequently denounced by various Mozambican leaders, has none the less proved to be extremely tenacious.

Another area of considerable innovation has been that of electoral law. The creation of popular assemblies at all the different levels of administrative organization has required a relatively elaborate set of rules governing the qualifications for electing and being elected and the procedures to be followed. In the early years, a notable feature of the electoral law was the exclusion from the suffrage of classes of persons who were regarded as being totally involved in the system of colonial oppression. This included members of the former secret police and other organizations directly associated with Portuguese fascism, but also extended to those persons who had acted as chiefs. Election was basically conducted by means of public assemblies with votes being counted by means of a show of hands. These assemblies had the virtue of confronting the electors and the elected face-to-face. It conformed to African tradition inasmuch as it personalized the procedures rather than detach the electors from the elected. In many of the electoral meetings, vigorous debates took place about the qualities of the candidates, and frequently in this way substantive political questions were raised and heartily discussed. The trend more recently, however, has been to seek ways to extend the principle of a secret ballot, and find new ways of encouraging public debate. While vigorous public discussion never became completely attenuated, its spontaneous character became increasingly less evident. The paradox emerged that Mozambicans felt free to speak out and voice their opinions on every occasion except those set aside for public debate. Another trend has been to eliminate bars to voting.

In the area of economic law, the changes have been equally dramatic. The first phase, which commenced in the short transitional period leading up to independence, was characterized by legislation principally designed to prevent the withdrawal of capital assets and the deliberate sabotaging of the economy. The second phase, which followed some years after independence, saw the creation of new economic enterprises, generally of a para-statal kind, based on the amalgamation of large numbers of small enterprises that had been abandoned by their owners or that had gone into insolvency. Special legislation was adopted dealing with the constitution, structure, functioning and norms of these economic enterprises, as well as of joint ventures that were to be established between foreign private capital and Mozambican state companies. At the same time, a law was passed dealing with the establishment and functioning of co-operatives. The co-operative sector has been important in certain areas of agricultural activity, particularly in the green belt around Maputo. Co-operatives were also established in the retail area and played an important role in the distribution of food and other commodities in short supply; these were called consumer co-operatives. At the same time, banking, insurance, export and import trade, the construction industry and the furnishing and letting of properties for rent, were effectively placed under state control. The third and more recent phase of economic law has seen the adoption of an extensive number of statutes designed to facilitate the investment of foreign capital in Mozambique and the stimulation of private initiative by Mozambican entrepreneurs themselves.

One of the most difficult areas for the legislators has been that relating to what some persons call the informal economic sector. The hopes that the informal sector would be taken over by the co-operative sector proved largely misplaced. In fact, the development of the war and the associated shortages (not all of which could be attributed simply to the war situation) gave rise to the development of black marketeering on a very large scale. This is referred to in the article dealing with the two aspects of socialist legality. There has been extensive debate and questioning on the issue of how best to deal with the black market, bearing in mind that it frequently had direct security as well as economic implications. In the period 1983–84, legislation was adopted in order to repress black marketeering as directly as possible. In particular, the use of whipping, heavy fines and imprisonment was introduced as a means of combating black marketeering. As part of a package designed to stiffen the legal system, the Law Faculty was suspended, a new Minister of Justice was nominated, and an attempt was made to utilize the criminal law as a major means of influencing economic activity. Readers of the article 'The Two Sides of Socialist Legality' will pick up the sense of distress which these measures induced in many of us. Were we simply privileged intellectuals hidebound by abstract concepts of human rights while the country was being engulfed by war and hunger? Were we completely out of touch with public opinion? Had the whole humanistic tradition, starting with the treatment of captured Portuguese soldiers during the independence struggle, been an illusion?

The questions shall remain, even though the climate today is completely different – the whipping law has been repealed, the Law Faculty has been reopened, and economic rather than penal measures are being used as the principal means of dealing with the black market (now often referred to as 'the parallel economy'). This has resulted in new legislation grouped together in what is referred to as the Economic Rehabilitation Programme. Characteristics of this legislation are: the progressive deregulation of prices, particularly those relating to agricultural production; the devaluation of the national currency in relation to international rates of exchange; and the emphasis on the creation of bodies which can represent the interests of small producers.

The penal laws used in an attempt to crack down on black marketeering together with legislation designed to deal directly with sabotage associated with the war, had considerable human rights implications which attracted the interest of international human rights organizations. At the time of the preparation of this introduction, there has been extensive dialogue between these organizations and the Mozambican government. In particular, Amnesty International sent a delegation to Mozambique, the leader of which declared that many earlier criticisms of the country had either been unsubstantiated or else had been overtaken by positive developments. It should be stressed that the papers in this book do not address themselves directly to the question of human rights. Nevertheless, in our capacity as personnel of the Department of Investigation and Legislation, we have frequently had to deal with these questions in relation to observations made by visitors to Mozambique and enquiries we received from abroad. What we feel should be underlined is that, important though respect for procedural safeguards always is, equally important is the establishment of an operative legal system that reaches into and responds to the needs of the community, applying principles that contain in their essence respect for the rights of all citizens. This is particularly important in relation to the question of family law which will be dealt with at a later stage.

As far as the questions raised in the paper on the two sides of socialist legality are concerned, we would like to point out that considerable attention is now being paid to the question of guaranteeing procedural rights of citizens and establishing what in general terms might be called the rule of law. If the article were to be re-written today, perhaps it would be entitled 'The Three Sides of Socialist Legality'. In other words, it would focus not simply on the tension between the liberating and freedom-enhancing aspects of community-based law on the one hand, and the necessity to defend the gains of independence and the new society on the other, but also raise a third dimension by insisting on the application of what some refer to as internationally accepted norms of justice. This third dimension comes in partly as a result of international attention focused on Mozambique, but principally because of an insistence on the part of Mozambicans themselves that there be clearly defined and understood criteria governing the rights of persons faced with being deprived of their liberty. The attempts to control abuses committed by those wearing the uniform of authority have to be based fundamentally on community awareness, proper selection and training of those in authority, and a general extension of respect for the law by means of campaigns of public education. But our experiences suggest that the development of a properly functioning court structure and the creation of a strong set of legal counsel, together with the adoption of clear laws, also have a crucial role to play.

Socialist legality in this sense becomes less rather than more demarcated from bourgeois legality. This is a theme that requires considerable reflection and one which will surely occupy the minds of all legal thinkers in Mozambique for many years to come. The argument would be that certain procedural rights and guarantees, commonly referred to as human rights or respect for human rights, constitute part of the patrimony of humankind as a whole, having been achieved as the result of struggles in many parts of the world over long periods of time with extensive popular involvement. As such, far from being the exclusive property of one form of social organization, they can and should be incorporated into the philosophy and practice of all societies, however organized. We might mention in passing that the very definition of Mozambique as a socialist country has also been under debate; not inasmuch as there are direct attempts to change the character of the society into an avowedly capitalist one, but insofar as the question is being raised as to whether it was possible to leap directly from the colonial capitalist society into an independent socialist society without first passing through various intermediate stages involving a mixed economy and the gradual unfolding of what is called the democratic revolution.

These are controversial questions that have implications going well beyond Mozambique. Where we do express ourselves more confidently is in relation to the evolution of the law in relation to the family in Mozambique.

In any part of the world, family law is people's law. Nowhere is this more so the case than in an underdeveloped country. The core of the papers in this book in fact relates to questions raised by family law in Mozambique. It is here that the tension between the old and the new, the traditional and the modern, the conservative and the evolutionary, presents itself in its most striking and, at the same time, in its most intimate form. It raises the whole question of imposed law versus indigenous law and goes directly to the heart of the functioning of the courts. In our view, this is the area of most significant legal transformation made in Mozambique. The experience needs to be closely studied since it has extensive and interesting implications for socio-legal development anywhere in Africa, and for that matter, anywhere in the Third World. Certainly this is the area in which popular justice has had its greatest success.

Down with *lobolo*! Down with polygamy! Down with child marriages! In the years immediately after independence, no meeting anywhere in the country and on any theme was complete without a denunciation of what were considered the three great evils of traditional family law. Today it is much rarer to hear such denunciations. While polygamy and child marriages are still frowned upon, there is much greater tolerance towards the institution of *lobolo* (the payment of bride wealth) which is seen as having considerable cultural relevance for the population. The trend has been away from complete and unconditional attack towards criticizing the exploitative aspects of the institution while recognizing its tenacity and meaning for the people. Similarly, in relation to initiation rites, there has been a move away from denouncing them as backward and feudal. The two aspects which are condemned are mutilation and the training of women to be inferior, respectively. For the rest, initiation rites are seen as constituting an important means of promoting civic and sexual education, especially in the countryside. The fact remains, however, that considerable transformation has taken place in respect of the concept of the family and the kinds of intervention which the courts will make. Thus, while *lobolo* continues to be widely paid and to have considerable significance in the setting up of new families and the ways in which property is distributed after death or on the break-up of marriage, it is not formally recognized by the courts, and does not constitute a source of law.

The remarkable achievement of the community courts operating at the level of the grassroots 'from the Rovuma to the Maputo' has been to establish as an operational fact the uniformity of family law throughout the country. In a society with so many different languages, religions, and traditional methods of constituting the family, this is something worth studying in some detail. From our observations, we can say that this is not simply a case of a law that exists on paper in the name of nation-building but which is ignored in practice. Thousands of judges every week hear cases involving matrimonial disputes, and the research that we have done indicates that in fundamental outline, the procedures and principles which are adopted are essentially the same independently of whether the family in crisis had been set up in the context of a Christian marriage ceremony, an Islamic one, or by means of payment of *lobolo*. A vast system of informal or non-state law clearly continues to exist side by side with the state law. But the state courts, consisting of judges drawn directly from the local community, are bombarded with cases referred to them by citizens in the neighbourhood unable to resolve their problems by informal means. This is particularly important as far as women's rights are concerned. One might say that, in general terms, the courts operate to balance out to a considerable extent the advantages which men enjoy in the society at large, advantages of (normally) greater physical strength and economic power, and the superiority attributed to them by tradition. The fact that the courts usually include at least one woman, and that in most areas where the courts function, the Organization of Mozambican Women (OMM) also operates, has had a significant effect on changing practices and values.

Mozambique has opted for a unitarian rather than a pluralistic legal approach in a country marked by extensive cultural diversity. In recent years, our department has been called upon to conduct research which required us to investigate this very question. In the late 1970s, a draft of a new family law code was elaborated which incorporated the fundamental constitutional principles of equality between men and women as part of its foundation. In essence, the family law code accepted two types of divorce, namely, litigious divorce and divorce by mutual consent based on one year's separation. In the case of litigious divorce, the court had to make a finding as to whether there had been a complete collapse of the family. A feature of the draft was the extensive recognition given to unregistered marriages, i.e., to family unions recognized by the community at large as marriages, but which had not been registered with the civil authorities. Research which we had done indicated that probably about ninety per cent of all marriages in Mozambique were not registered. Thus the recognition given to what were called *de facto* unions meant that the principles of the draft family code could be extended to the population as a whole. A directive from the Judge President of the Superior Court of Appeal put certain key sections of the draft family code into effect (1982). In particular, the directive recognized that *de facto* unions could be recognized and treated by the courts essentially as though they were registered marriages. The directive also established new criteria and procedures for divorce, thereby completely replacing large portions of the family law section of the Civil Code. The task given to our department was to do fresh research re-examining the draft, creating thereby the basis for the production of a new family law code for the country.

The research was conducted in all the provinces and resulted in a report which is presently being studied by the Government. What was of greatest interest to us was the opinions that were expressed by the hundreds of persons we interviewed in relation to the general question of whether or not to recognize the rules of customary law in the courts.

The question was not put in an abstract way as to whether the interviewees supported a unitary or a pluralistic legal system, but concretely as to whether the courts should apply the traditional rules in relation to *lobolo*, Muslim marriages and so on. The answers received from all parts of the country were virtually unanimous – the persons consulted did not wish to see the diverse rules of customary law incorporated into the decisions of the courts. What they did want was greater sensitivity on the part of the legal system to certain general aspects of tradition. Thus they wished to see more involvement of parents in questions of both marriage and divorce. As far as marriage was concerned, they accepted the right of persons who had achieved the age of majority to marry at will without necessarily getting the consent of their parents or guardians. What they did insist on, however, was that the parents or guardians be consulted before such marriage takes place and be given the opportunity to offer their counsel. Similarly, in relation to divorce, the interviewees recognized that the decision as to whether or not to grant the divorce lay exclusively with the court, but they felt strongly that there should be a compulsory reference by the court to the parents or guardians with a view to ascertaining their opinions. Another interesting fact which emerged from our research was that the persons interviewed wished, in cases of a divorce, that a finding be made as to which of the parties was the guilty one, subject to the rider that such a finding would not affect questions of custody of the children or distribution of the matrimonial assets.

Another aspect that aroused strong feelings was that of adoption. As a result of the war and destabilization imposed on Mozambique, tens of thousands of children have been orphaned or torn from their families. A major effort is under way to place these children in foster homes, and the question arises as to whether they should be legally adopted or not. When we put this matter in the questionnaire, the almost unanimous response of the interviewees was against formal adoption if that meant that the children were to be completely cut off from their biological parents. In general, we found that there was strong cultural resistance to the idea of adoption if this legal institution involved the complete substitution of the new family for the birth family of the child. This was shocking in a double sense, in that it presupposed that there was no one from the wider family willing to look after the child, and, second, that if the day arrived when the child discovered a member of the family to which he or she had been tied by birth, he or she would be unable to restore its legal links. The proposal that emerged from the enquiry was that a form of adoption be recognized in which the child entered the new home and took on all the rights and responsibilities of a child of that family, without completely severing his or her ties with the birth family. Thus, if one day the family of the child's birth was able to establish a connection with the child, or the child with the family, the adoption would be modified to that extent. This is a good example of introducing what is a very widely accepted legal institution, that is, one accepted in many parts of the world, into an African context in a way in which account would be taken of African cultural tradition without voiding the institution completely of its substance.

In the light of the research done, and the scepticism of the Africanist scholars notwithstanding, we stand by our opinion that the unitary rather than pluralist policy towards the Mozambican legal system has been the appropriate one. The article entitled 'Beyond Pluralism' was prepared for a conference in Nairobi, the main thrust of which was to have more rather than less respect for legal pluralism. Our paper therefore went against the mainstream. It is evident that much more dialogue is required on the subject. Clearly we oppose attempts to create a steam-rollered national unity which is totally insensitive to the variety of life-styles and multiplicity of beliefs and practices of the people. (It does not work, anyway.) But in the case of Mozambique, pluralism is associated with colonial domination and the creation of different levels of citizenship. The idea of national unity, and the importance of the struggle against racism, tribalism and regionalism, were fundamental to the prosecution of the fight for independence, and in the post-independence period have played an equally important role in enabling the country to resist destabilization and aggression. The underlying approach has always been that it was not colonialism which created the country, but the struggle – within boundaries created by colonialism – against foreign domination. Today the struggle is for development and against war and hunger, and once more the theme of national unity is central. What our research showed was that this is a theme that has entered public consciousness and directly affects the choices that the public makes. The correctness of a unitary approach in Mozambique relates to the particular history of the country, to the existence of the liberated zones and the swift collapse of the system of chieftaincy. It does not mean that it is appropriate for other countries in Africa that might have had quite different processes of creation and development.

In looking at the various articles in this book dealing with the rights of women, the reader should bear in mind that the war, which is not directly referred to in these articles, has had a significant impact on the role of Mozambican women in the larger society. This is so not simply because literally millions of women have had their lives disrupted by the war, but because women are actively engaged in dealing with its aftermath. This is a sad addition to the principle that the liberation of women requires their involvement in the major tasks confronting the nation. In practice, women are involved extensively in the question of relief, not so much in relation to the distribution of food, but rather in respect of helping to restore as normal a life as possible to displaced people and, in particular, in caring for the children whose lives have been disrupted by the war. This requires extensive mobilization and the principal activists in this area, just as they were during the national independence war, are the women of the rural areas.

The war affects every aspect of life in the country, the legal system no less than any other. Sometimes the effect is direct, as for example when the war reaches a village and the judges, together with other persons in the area, are forced to move. Frequently, the impact is indirect, such as when shortages are created because of the enormous cost of the war. Thus, there is a shortage of petrol and prisoners are requested to walk sometimes several miles and without escort from their awaiting-trial prisons to the courthouse. Or the problem might be a shortage of paper, which holds up the publication of legislation. The impact reaches into the heart of the society, affecting methods and styles of work. The essay, 'The Two Dimensions of Socialist Legality' has to be read against the background of the war. It was the war which created the shortages or aggravated the shortages which had already emerged because of the whole process of transformation and the problems of management which inevitably occurred. It was the war which distracted the attention of the leaders from the problems of development and reconstruction and created an atmosphere of prolonged and deep crisis in the country. It was the war which destroyed rural infrastructures, made circulation in the country difficult, and prevented the gradual extension of services which had been implicit in many of the immediate post-independence plans.

Since the essay on socialist legality was written, an important change in style of work has taken place in the country. At that time, there was considerable emphasis on active intervention both as a means of defending the gains of the revolutionary process and as a way of dealing with abuses that had arisen in the course of that process. The closing down of the Law Faculty and the introduction of the whipping law should be seen as two examples of that approach. Considerable emphasis was put on the element of consciousness, of organized enthusiasm. Mobilization, mass meetings, the direct intervention of leading personnel by means of visits to affected areas, were all major means of dealing with crises and inertia. At present, we find ourselves in a substantially different plane of work. The emphasis now is far less on direct intervention and far more on the gradual building of basic infrastructures, the encouragement of local and individual initiative, and a policy that regards the State as providing the broad framework for economic and social activity, rather than as being the immediate directing agent. This has had significant implications for the legal system and the application of penal law. As has been mentioned, instead of dealing with the black market primarily through punishing black marketeers, an attempt has been made to combat it by economic measures. This has involved the deregulation of prices in the market, the increase in the prices paid to producers and the involvement of the private sector (in particular of the small family private sector) in the production and distribution of basic commodities. To take one concrete example of the new approach: instead of attempting to deal with the problem of pirate transport by means of applying the criminal law, attempts have been made to bring this so-called informal sector of economic activity under some form of regulation. The idea is that where the public sector fails to provide sufficient transport for the population, it would be inappropriate to attempt to penalize those persons in possession of transport who use their cars and lorries as a means of carrying goods and persons to and fro, even if at high prices. Concretely, this means that such pirate taxis should be registered wherever possible, given supplies of petrol, and required to submit to basic safety regulations.

At the same time, attempts are made to strengthen the legal system by means of an accelerated programme of training. The Law Faculty is reopened and students continue with their studies where they left off before. A number of young Mozambican lawyers are sent abroad for post-graduate study. Attempts are being made to constitute a Mozambican bar. This is not easy. The basic problem is to reconcile the need to have a strong and independent bar as one of three pillars of the justice system, while at the same time avoiding the kind of liberalization of the profession that would result in only the rich getting legal services. The National Institute of Legal Aid is established to group together all the lawyers available to appear in court or offer legal advice. It agrees on its statutes and on its tariff of fees, but it still takes time to establish a clear profile of the lawyer in a newly independent and under-developed country committed to building socialism. The country as a whole is passing through a phase of extensive re-examination and reflection. It is not so much the commitment to socialism which is under review, but how best to achieve it, and what aspects of past policies need to be corrected, and which need to be reinforced. Clearly, this debate has implications for the evolution of the legal system. At the same time, the legal system has to respond to the many demands placed upon it, and has to expand and evolve, without necessarily waiting for final decisions on the wider questions. What is very noticeable is that great emphasis is being placed on the evolution of the legal system in the direction of making it more compatible with what are regarded as international norms of procedure and due process. In other words, the fact that Mozambique regards itself as a revolutionary society, or at least as a society undergoing profound transformations, is less and less of a reason for having extraordinary courts and extraordinary procedures. Thus, less emphasis is put on the originality or even uniqueness of the Mozambican experience, and more on its adherence to universal norms.

Thus the evolving situation, the debate on how to characterize the present phase of evolution of Mozambican society, and the new style in methods of work, all affect both faces of socialist legality. On the one hand, there is far less emphasis on the use of penal measures as a means of securing the gains of the revolution. On the other, the question of how best to secure the individual rights of citizens and how best to eliminate abuses of authority is being tackled far less from an interventionist perspective and far more from the basis of building the structures of the legal system itself. To take one vivid example, the awaiting trial prisons of Maputo have been chronically and grossly overcrowded with prisoners. In the earlier years, attempts were made to deal with this problem by means of emergency sessions of the courts, with the judges working nights and weekends to clear the backlog. More recently, however, the approach has been to establish district courts that can relieve the High Court of its enormous case-load. Within two years, the awaiting trial time has been cut by well over 50 per cent. Quiet planning and proper follow-through achieved what years of sudden mobilizations and appeals to consciousness had failed to do.

It is not difficult to offer firm but banal reflections and conclusions. Thus the major problems appear to us now to be as they have always been.

First, there is the problem of the relationship between the popular and the professional. Undoubtedly the major contribution and area of originality of the Mozambican legal system has been in relation to its popular or community involvement. But to what extent does this popular involvement in any society claiming to be revolutionary or progressive, have to be affected or disciplined by professionalism? Our experience suggests that both the popular and the professional aspects have to be developed simultaneously. It is not simply a question of balance, that is, of balancing out the popular aspects with professionalism and the professional aspects with community involvement. There has to be a clear understanding of the kinds of work issues to be tried, their level of seriousness and the consequences of the trial for the litigants and for the society at large. Thus, when it comes to dealing with the large number of family disputes, neighbours' quarrels, crimes of petty hooliganism and so on, without doubt the wholly elected popular tribunals at the grassroots level have functioned exceptionally well. This does not mean that the same kind of court operating in the same kind of way would be appropriate for a charge of murder or treason or rape. In the case of these crimes, where the penalties may be severe and deprivation of liberty involved, there is a great need for the application of clearly established principles contained in proper criminal codes, and for the matter to be adjudicated upon by a team of persons including at least one professionally trained judge. Most important of all, proper legal defence has to be made available to the accused in such matters. This is not just a question of bowing to international pressures, or of attempting to copy the better aspects of the erstwhile colonial legal system. Large sections of the population of the country itself feel and indicate that they wish to have secure procedures when it comes to questions of imprisonment.

There might be argument about whether one can speak of an innate sense of justice, or about whether there are certain procedures which fundamentally correspond to the nature of human beings. The fact is that through cultural diffusion, allied to the kinds of demands that are expressed by peoples engaged in struggles for independence and development, certain notions have become part and parcel of the consciousness of people in Mozambique, as in other countries. It might be that very few black Mozambicans in colonial times had any positive experience of the courts, and that because of the fascist character of Portugal itself, and despite the existence of a small number of progressive lawyers and judges, the legal system had relatively little prestige even amongst the colonists. The fact is, however, that through literature, television, radio and other means of mass communication, the concept of a fair trial, with objective appreciation by the judges and the possibilities of a vigorous defence on behalf of the accused, has become extensively acknowledged and regarded as desirable. The Mozambican revolution does not make itself more attractive to the population by distancing itself from these notions in the name of revolutionary or popular justice. On the contrary, it appears to the people that, in the name of the revolution, they are being deprived of something which a so-called normal society would have. The problem facing those who wish sincerely and profoundly to transform the colonial-type structures of justice and replace them with new structures that clearly serve the interests of the people, is precisely how to create the conditions both institutionally and subjectively for the integration of these so-called universal standards of justice into a popular community-based system. The choice need not be between the extremes of a system based simply on the application of what one might call the general will, that is, of de-professionalizing completely legal procedures and ensuring that the popular element monopolizes decision making, or a system based exclusively on abstruse codes and complicated procedures that can only be operated by a professional caste remote from the people and seeking to advance its own power and wealth through its monopoly of forensic skills and information. It should be possible, indeed it appears to us to be absolutely essential, to continue to draw heavily on community involvement, especially at the grassroots level, so as to maintain an open and accessible character to the law in terms of its formulation and diffusion, while at the same time ensuring a necessary professional ingredient to guarantee proper procedures in the more serious cases, and to give a sense of seriousness and discipline to the legal structure as a whole.

These need not be antagonistic tendencies. On the contrary, our experience has been that the community court judges welcome all the support they can get from professional judges and, in fact, demand more rather than less orientation. At the same time, the professional judges find that where the courts are functioning well, the participation of elected judges aids them considerably in arriving at just results. The professional judges need to be drawn from all sectors of the population and to have a kind of training that will make them naturally sensitive and responsive to the problems at the grassroots level. At the same time, high degrees of professional skill should be required of them in appropriate types of cases, for example, in complicated international business transactions.

The second banality is that one of the fundamental problems continues to be the relationship between preserving all that is positive in African tradition while transforming society at its roots. Here again, we feel that in relation to the community courts and the evolution of family law, Mozambique has made a notable contribution. Whether the changes introduced should be called socialist or national democratic transformation, or simply nation-building or modernization, they do amount to a significant change in the way things are done and the way people see themselves. In our view, the success of the community courts as the most vibrant, innovative, and perhaps substantial part of the popular justice system derives precisely from the fact that they harmonize well with fundamental features of African tradition, while completely transforming that tradition. Thus, the question poses itself not so much as one of purging or eliminating what are regarded as negative aspects of African tradition, but of allowing the vital and democratic aspects to flourish in the context of the new and developing society. The tradition of extensive popular involvement in the resolution of disputes can be transformed relatively easily into the foundations of the new system applying new values.

A third banality is that it is crucial to establish the correct relationship between formal and informal legal systems, that is, between the formal state sector and the vast area of dispute settlement that takes place in the community in an informal way. The state sector at its best should represent all that is new, that transforms, that helps to establish a new consciousness. But it should not be seen as an exclusive domain that can only survive by means of suppressing other forms of settling disputes. It could be that the specific characteristic of the Mozambican revolution in eliminating rather than reviving or integrating the system of chieftainship, was a fundamental prerequisite for the establishment of a truly national form of popular justice. It might be that in many other societies undergoing profound transformation, traditional politics and traditional structures could play a greater role than they have in the case of Mozambique. In such a situation, the relationship between the formal and the informal sectors becomes even more problematic. Should the judicial functioning of the traditional tribal or religious authorities be incorporated into the formal state sector, or should it be simply tolerated outside of it, or should it be slowly, or rapidly, suppressed? What is highly relevant in the Mozambican case is that the destruction of the system of chieftaincy that followed the destruction of the old colonial administration resulted in the possibilities of incorporating the traditional forms of popular participation in judicial matters into the formal state structure, while allowing the informal application of traditional rules to continue outside of that structure. What was important was that the rules which had been applied by the chiefs, the power that the judicial authority gave them, the emphasis on ethnicity and the caste-like structure that divided the royals from the commoners, were eliminated.

The final banality is that it is necessary to resolve the tension between reliance on purely indigenous forms of training and organization and the utilization of external supports. By indigenous in this context one does not mean traditional. The Mozambican revolutionary process was an indigenous one that involved millions of people, and which threw up new institutions and ways of seeing and doing things. It was original, African and modernizing all in one. The stronger the indigenous process, and the more profound its roots, the more it was able to benefit from outside support. In our own area relating to the community courts, we found this very much to be the case. Once when one of us was explaining to a North American audience how the popular justice system first took root, with a series of pilot schemes in each province, one commentator unkindly pointed out that they sounded exactly like a Ford Foundation project except that the latter never got beyond the pilot scheme. In fact, at the foundation stage, all the work was done without the benefit of any international funding or project aid. We are happy to say, however, that at a later stage, together with the Norwegian agency for development (NORAD), the Ford Foundation contributed substantially towards the materialization of many of the goals of the Department of Research and Legislation. Our experience was that project aid could not really be useful in the establishment of goals and the laying of the foundations of the new legal system, but at a later stage could be immensely valuable in the fulfilment of objectives that had already been clearly established, and in particular as a means of furthering the more interesting and experimental aspects of our work. We should mention that the preparation and production of this book owes a lot to both organizations.

Far more difficult than stating these rather banal antinomies is to evaluate in an overall way the achievements and failures of the process of transforming the legal system. What criteria are to be applied? Should one set the achievements against the goals so confidently and clearly expressed in the early years after independence? Or should one question some of these goals themselves? The greatest problem lies not so much in evaluating the legal system itself, but in evaluating the Mozambican revolutionary process as a whole. This broader type of analysis and inquiry is at present being extensively conducted in the country in all sorts of ways and at all sorts of levels. It goes well beyond the scope of this modest introduction. It is clear that it is impossible to evaluate the successes and failures of transforming the legal system without doing so in the context of a wide evaluation of the whole process of transforming Mozambique. At the same time, the global evaluation has to take into account a stock-taking in relation to the particular parts. We hope therefore that this book serves some purpose in enabling people, inside and outside Mozambique, to evaluate the significance of steps that have been taken in the years since independence to transform the life of the country and overcome the immense difficulties inherited from the past.

Our synoptic assessment in relation to the legal system would be that, in its fundamental aspects, the system of popular justice has proved itself enduring and valuable and capable of being put into effective operation, but that at the same time it has required substantial adaptations and modifications, most of which have pointed in the direction of reinforcing what might be called internationally accepted procedures, values, and methods of training. Similarly, the content and objectives of the law have undergone a process of adaptation which has made them more in accord with, rather than disruptive of, what might be referred to as internationally accepted types of law. Whether this flows from the fact that in reality there is a global patrimony of legal forms and ideas which can be utilized as well by countries intending to build socialism as by countries which are avowedly capitalist in nature, or whether it represents a capitulation to the powerful embrace of capitalist ideas and ways of doing things, remains to be seen.

July 1989

1. Liberating the Land, Liberating the Law*

Introduction

It is no surprise that many lawyers regard the very notion of revolutionary legality with total suspicion. In their view either law annihilates the revolution, or the revolution annihilates the law. Yet the actual experience of the People's Republic of Mozambique suggests that the relationship between law and revolution is one of mutual interdependence rather than one of mutual destruction, and that if indeed the revolution does abolish one type of legal order it is only to replace it with another. The revolution uses law to fight law, it establishes totally new sets of assumptions and procedures and it creates a whole new legal style. But in destroying old law it gives birth to new law, which locks itself in combat not with the revolution – which is its creator – but with the old which it replaces.

This essay will attempt by means of a study of a concrete piece of legislation to show how law and revolution serve each other. The statute chosen is the *Mozambican Land Law*,[1] adopted by the People's Assembly in 1979, four years after independence, a piece of legislation which can quite fairly be classified as revolutionary, both in its content and in its format.

When introducing the *Law* to the Assembly, the Minister of Justice pointed out that the land was restored to the people of Mozambique not through land reform but through revolution. The result of this is that the *Land Law* is not designed essentially as an instrument to promote social change, but rather as a means of guaranteeing changes that have already taken place; the law is not contemplated as the means of maintaining the primacy of the interests of the class alliance in power.

The fundamental principle of the *Land Law* is that the land cannot be alienated. With one legislative stroke, the vast mass of colonial legislation dealing with title to land is eliminated. Land law passes from private law to public law. Real rights in land disappear, and property law becomes essentially the law of movables; that is, essentially the law of ownership and use of consumer goods. The textbooks on land law, which deal essentially with the

* An earlier version of this paper, originally prepared by Albie Sachs, was published by the Institute of African Studies, Harvard University, 1980.

demarcation of boundaries, the determination of title and the conjugation of various interests in relation to the same piece of territory, become obsolete. Land is withdrawn from the market. It can no longer serve as a security, can no longer be seized to satisfy a debt. If, historically speaking, it took a revolution to destroy the traditional-feudal fetters that kept land from the market, now it has taken another revolution to make land inalienable once more, but this time inalienable because it belongs to the nation as a whole, and not because it is tied by feudal lineage to certain families or class.

In keeping with the notion of 'popular justice', the law is not only written in clear and accessible language but also published in inexpensive pamphlet form with large type in Portuguese so that it may be widely consulted. The pamphlet includes the text of the law, the Minister's introductory speech, and an official *Explanatory Note*. Perhaps even more than the text itself, this Note indicates the kind of thinking that went into the preparation of the law, and for this reason the Note will be reproduced *in extenso* to serve as the basis for the commentary on Law and Revolution which will follow.

The Official Explanatory Note to the Mozambican Land Law: An Overview[2]

The *Land Law*, approved during the Fourth Ordinary Session of the Popular Assembly, sets out to define the fundamental principles regulating the use and benefit of land, as well as the forms that these may take in the People's Republic of Mozambique.

Land law derives its importance from two basic causes. The first is of a general order – land is one of the principal means of production at man's disposal and has played a fundamental role throughout the history of humanity, the system of its appropriation or utilization being an essential element in the characterization of the level of development of societies. The second is of a more particular character – after the repeal of colonial legislation on this topic, brought about by Article 8 of the Constitution, the *Land Law* replaces the older systems of appropriating and utilizing the land of our country with a new type of control.

These two reasons convey the importance and the necessity of studying this law. For a correct analysis of the law, we must first understand the role that land has played in the various phases of the process of domination and colonial exploitation in Mozambique.

a) Colonial Expansion

The so-called expansion of 'Faith and Empire' that served as the banner of Portuguese colonialism had from its very beginning a precise economic objective: to subject people to political domination so as better to exploit them. In the beginning the principal treasure and object of exploitation was man himself, stripped of his human condition and exported as merchandise to the Americas. Portugal, thus, was one of the principal emporiums of slavery, indulging in a trade that was responsible for the depopulation of large areas of the African continent. Later when the European powers lost their colonial dominance in the Americas, they turned to Africa with a view to exploiting its riches by utilizing the manual labour they had ceased to export. Thus began the effective occupation of the territories into which they divided the continent for themselves.

In this phase colonialism proceeded in two ways: on the one hand the most fertile lands were appropriated, pushing the population to the unproductive zones where only a precarious agricultural subsistence was possible; and on the other hand taxes were levied, at a level which was beyond the possible income of these less productive lands. Men had to work on plantations where they received miserable salaries, devised in such a way that the period of work necessary to earn a sufficient amount to pay the tax would not be a short one. This was one of the pillars of the system of forced labour imposed on Mozambicans.

For whom were these lands destined? In some regions of the country they were converted into *prazos* (leased lands) and given by means of a feudal system to *prazeiros* (land lease recipients). Later there arose the so-called royal companies that were capitalist corporations with interests in various countries, to whom the colonial power ceded sovereignty over extensive regions. In these territories the royal companies coined their own money and levied their own taxes, organizing at their own cost total economic exploitation of the area in exchange for a set payment to the Portuguese State. Such, for example, were the cases of the Company of Zambezia and the Company of Niassa. On the other hand, great plantations arose and developed at the cost of further usurpation of lands.

This history of conquest of pillage and of violence to serve the ends of exploitation, was the principal element characterizing the phase of implantation of the Portuguese colonial system in Mozambique. This was the basis of the entire process of primitive accumulation of capital which was to occur later.

b) Land Occupation

In more recent times and in face of mounting criticism of colonialism, the colonial-facist regime, not losing sight of its goal of an even more systematic exploitation, concerned itself with the problem of presenting a more acceptable image. It is thus that the *Regulation of the Occupation and Concession of the Lands of the Overseas Provinces* – legislation which gave the colonial state and the colonists the legal instruments with which to plunder (African) populations and occupy their lands – also purported, in a hypocritical gesture, to achieve the 'intransigent defence of the interests and the right of the [African] populations on the lands occupied and exploited by them.'

It is useful to remember some of its principal dispositions. The lands were classified in terms of their quality, or by their value, in the following way:

- first class lands: these were the lands that included the so-called classified settlements and suburbs inhabitated by the colonists;

– second class lands: these were set aside for the people, up to a fifth of the area occupied by each administrative office;
– third class lands: these were the so-called vacant lands that belonged neither to the first class nor the second class.

The first and third class were subject to concession, being acquired under the same right of definitive property duly titled – these were the lands destined for the colonial state and the colonists. Second class lands, destined for indigenous natives, later called *vizinhos de regedoria* (neighbours of the administration) or simply *autoctones* (autochthons), were not subject to the right of individual title.

The above *Regulation* provided that the concessions be gratuitous in the case of settlers or 'national Catholic missions'. In the latter case they could include areas of up to two thousand hectares, this concessionary right being established by the Missionary Accord of 1940 between Portugal and the Holy See. This is just one example of the way the Church was entangled with Portuguese colonialism. With the necessity of defending itself from the criticisms which increasingly exposed the system, Portuguese colonialism went in for the hypocritical and demagogic device of prohibiting 'under the penalty of sanction the movement of populations to lands different from those they occupied with the intention of including them, in whole or part, within provisional boundaries.' This provision did no more than pretend to rid the State of responsibility for the violent seizure of lands that the companies and colonists proceeded to accomplish in systematic fashion, with the direct connivance of the colonial structures, the Administrator, the Geographical Register services and, at the top, the Provincial Secretary for Population. Together, they always prompted or provided the necessary politico-legal cover for these actions. Consequently, it becomes clear that the entire system was based upon the expropriation of almost all useful land in the country which was simply declared to be 'empty lands' – that is, land belonging to no one. To those who had once been the original owners of all Mozambique's land, only one-fifth of the areas occupied by the administrative authority remained so-called second class lands.

c) The Armed Struggle for National Liberation

It was against this state of affairs that the flames of resistance arose and always kept burning. This was resistance against the occupation of land and against the subjection of persons on it to foreign domination.

When the Central Committee of Frelimo proclaimed a general armed uprising against Portuguese colonialism on 25 September 1964, the central objective was, right from the start, the liberation of the land and of the people on it from the domination and exploitation to which they had been subjected. This was a battle which would not end until the complete and total liquidation of this domination and exploitation had been achieved.

It was thus that in the Act of proclaiming independence on 25 June 1975, the *Constitution of the People's Republic of Mozambique* established that 'the land

and natural resources situated in the soil and in the subsoil, in the territorial waters, and in the Continental Shelf of Mozambique, are the property of the State' – of the workers' and peasants' State. In this way one of the central objectives of the liberation struggle was achieved, and the blood shed throughout generations was redeemed – the sacrifice of the nationalist fighters – and one of the most profound aspirations of all of the Mozambican people was realized: to restore to themselves ownership of the land.

The recuperation of the land by the Mozambican people is not a logical or natural consequence of the independence of the country. In many countries that have been independent for decades we do not witness the transfer of land from the colonialists to the hands of the people. In most cases reforms occur that tend to adapt colonial law and customary law to the new situation in which a national bourgeoisie replaces a colonial bourgeoisie. For us the recovery of the land is integral to the process of the Mozambican revolution. Because of this it can never signify the mere substitution of names on property titles nor the return to forms of appropriation and usage peculiar to feudal tradition. Accordingly, the recovery of the land by the people signifies the abolition once and for all of private ownership of land. The State of the worker and peasant alliance becomes the sole owner of the land which, in turn, becomes the patrimony of all of the people.

Article 8 of the *Constitution* constituted one of the first new acts of the revolution taking place after the process of taking power by the Mozambican working classes had been completed. Later, other measures followed within the context of the revolutionary programme, such as the nationalization of education, of medicine and of properties for rent. These and other measures formed the material and ideological bases of a socialist society and constituted on an economic and legal plane the instruments for the building of socialism.

The Purpose: What was the Land Law Intended to Achieve?

The above introduction gives us the historical context in which the *Land Law* arose, as well as its significance on the political, economic and legal planes. In this second part we shall proceed to analyse and characterize the principal elements and provisions of this *Law* with a view to understanding its mode of application. The simplest way would be to respect the continuity of the text, chapter by chapter, starting with the preamble.

a) Preamble

The function of the preamble is to explain in precise terms the historical origins of the *Law* and its importance on the political, economic and ideological planes. Thus, our introduction is a development of the ideas contained in the preamble.

b) Chapter I. General Dispositions

This chapter defines the fundamental principles upon which the remaining provisions of the *Law* as well as of any future regulations are dependent. Article 2 to Article 10 enunciate the fundamental concepts that materialize the principle that the land is the property of the State and that the State determines the conditions for its use and benefit.

Let us look at each of these underlying concepts:

i) Inalienability

The primary result of the principle that the land is the property of the State is that it cannot be sold. This prohibition is absolute: that is, neither citizens nor the State can sell land. Thus, land is inalienable.

Land cannot be rented, mortgaged or seized for payment. These were burdens on land possibly only in the case of private property ownership. What did they consist of?

– a rent consists of giving land for exploitation for a determined period of time in exchange for a payment, rent;
– a mortage consists of giving land as a guarantee for paying a debt. In case of non-payment, the creditor can be paid up to the value of the land;
– a seizure consists of the taking of goods so that with their value a debt may be satisfied.

These methods were eliminated with the abolition of private ownership of land.

ii) The right to work the land

Article I establishes the principle that all Mozambicans have the right to work the land, to live from it and to take from it the riches of their own efforts. This concept flows from the application of the principle that the land is the patrimony of the people. Later we shall see how this right is materialized.

iii) State Land Fund

The idea of a State Land Fund is derived from the consideration that, with all land belonging to the State, it is necessary to organize it in such a way that at any given moment the extent of usage can be known. The State Land Fund gives an account of the usage of all land that comprises the national territory.

iv) Classification

The *Land Law* utilizes the following two classifications:

- economic criterion: lands for agrarian purposes, lands for non-agrarian purposes.
– preservation criterion: totally protected lands, partly protected lands.

What is the value of this classification? This classification has the advantage of delimiting the more important aspects for regulation from the perspective of a land law. The criterion for the classification of land into land for agrarian purposes and land for non-agrarian purposes is an economic criterion distinguishing the two by function: for their use for agriculture, livestock and forestry on one hand, and industry, commerce, habitation and other purposes on the other.

The criterion that distinguishes land between totally protected land and partially protected land rests in the necessity to preserve areas for specific needs that range from military defence to the protection of communication systems, historical or national monuments, flora and fauna, and the like. Here the use of the land, whenever permitted, cannot run counter to the purpose for which it is protected.

The rights of use and benefit given to citizens as a result of this classification will tend to be for agrarian or non-agrarian purposes. The partially or totally protected reserves will always be established in favour of the interests of the State.

v) Titleholders or rights of use and benefit and licence

Each individual or collective person possessing legal capacity may be a titleholder to the right of use and benefit. That is, individuals or entities with legal personality such as associations, corporations, state companies, co-operatives, and the like may utilize the land under the terms of this law.

Titleholders have the right to utilize the land to produce wealth according to an approved plan for development. Beyond the principal aims written into this plan, they must in addition realize complementary or secondary objectives. Such is the case of a sugar company as titleholder which has the right of use and benefit for agrarian purposes of a given number of hectares of land designated for the cultivation of sugar cane; this company may also raise cattle or go in for other forms of farming, provided they represent ways of better benefiting from the lands.

Titleholders of the right of use and benefit have the following obligations:

- to utilize the lands in accordance with the plan for exploitation;
- to insure that their activities do not harm the State or other users;
- when lands are utilized for non-agrarian purposes, the users should make the lands suitable for agriculture after ending their usage for their initial purposes;
- to avoid wasting and erosion of the soil and to improve fertility;
- in the case of industrial companies, they should avoid the contamination and pollution of waters and of the land;
- to stop and prevent burnings, fires and destruction;
- to preserve and develop areas occupied by fruit trees and precious woods;
- to respect a period of three years of use in family farming before changing the land.

The violation of these obligations may give rise to the payment of compensation to the State and to persons directly injured as a result, as well as to the possibility of a fine and imprisonment for the defendant.

These obligations define the new attitude that man must have toward the land. Because land is not an unlimited resource – on the contrary, it can be depleted, age and even die – it is necessary to observe a certain number of principles and precautions to insure its conservation and development. In this way, the land will provide for our generation and for future generations. Accordingly, it is necessary to mobilize the citizens into adopting an attitude toward the land that is characterized by the correct methods of utilization and benefit.

The right to use and benefit must be evidenced by a written document that is a licence, issued by the competent state organ. The sole exception that the law considers is the use and benefit for the purposes of the family economy.

vi) Free land, fees, and 'prazos' (leases)

The *Law* establishes cases where the utilization of land is without payment and not subject to lease. Outside of these cases, the utilization of land will be on payment; that is, a fee established by regulation will be levied. When utilization is subject to lease, this may be from five to fifteen years, with the possibility of renewal of the lease as well as revocation should reasons justify it.

c) Chapter II. Land for Agrarian Purposes

The *Law* classifies land destined for agriculture, livestock and forestry.

Lands for agrarian purposes are sub-divided into the following categories:

i) Zones for planned agrarian development correspond to those areas for which there exists a general plan for development. This is the case of the Agro-Industrial Complex of the Limpopo. The utilization of land in these zones must comply with the guidelines established in the respective plan. Because the implementation of plans can result in loss to family farmers and others in the area concerned, the *Law* establishes the principle of compensation to these persons. Compensation is justified because the cost of the plan should not be borne in particular by the inhabitants of the zone but must be supported by all those who will benefit from its results, that is, by the community represented by the State.

Outside of these zones, which until now number only a few, it is possible to utilize land subject to authorization in the interest of the national economy.

(ii) Family farming corresponds to land utilized by members of a household for production. However, when the household employs wage/labour, the exploitation can no longer be considered familiar and it can no longer benefit from being classified under this regime. This concept of family exploitation is the consequence of the principle that working on the land, as the universal means for the creation of wealth, is the right of all the Mozambican people. It is a class concept that is opposed to the exploitation of man by man. It is different, on the other hand, from the concept of subsistence economy installed by colonialism.

In the colonial period these family units had been reduced to an economy whose perspective was one of subsistence, due to the pillage of the more fertile lands. Today, they constitute the family sector, still responsible for a significant part of total agricultural production. Its perspective is one of integrating the co-operative sector within the process of the building of a socialist society. Thus, while the law guarantees the utilization of land without payment and without subjection of lease, it also promotes integration into co-operatives, one of the forms of socialist ownership.

In addition to these guarantees, the *Law* establishes obligations, already referred to, which relate in particular to the necessity to avoid burnings and destruction. There is also the duty to rotate the land every three years.

d) Chapter III. Lands for Non-Agrarian Purposes

These lands are destined for habitation, industry, commerce, cultural, sport and other non-agrarian activities.

The *Land Law* gives special emphasis to lands for urban centres, placing the utilization of the land for non-agrarian purposes within the respective urban planning schemes. Two zones of land linked to urban centres are established: first, zones for expansion – as the name indicates, destined for the planned growth of the urban centre; secondly, the green belt – integrated in the urban centre and the zone of expansion it is intended for agricultural livestock and socio-cultural activities, as well as for the protection of the environment.

The most important principle established in this chapter is that when construction or any other improvements to the land are made without licence in these zones or zones that are covered by urbanization plans, there is no right to compensation or indemnification when removed.

e) Chapter IV. Protected Zones

This chapter of the *Land Law* refers to zones that, in view of their intrinsic value or in pursuit of specified objectives, cannot be utilized by citizens. These zones are, first, the totally protected zones – only conservation activities are permitted in such zones. These may be established for the protection of soil, flora and fauna, such as the Gorongos and Zinave reserves, for defence and security, historical monuments, and the like. Secondly, there are the partially protected zones. These are zones where utilization and benefit of the land is permitted provided the purpose for which the reserves were constituted is respected. This is the case for the strip of land along highways and railroads where certain types of agricultural utilization are possible, which are compatible with the safety and maintenance of these means of communication.

f) Chapter V. Powers

This chapter enunciates some general principles as to the competence of state institutions regarding the matter of lands. Thus, we have first, the Executive City Council. Its jurisdiction is restricted to areas covered by urbanization plans. In this respect the Council may authorize the use and benefit of land or propose preliminary urban planning projects to the City Assembly. Secondly, the Executive District Council exercises the same jurisdiction in relation to areas covered by urbanization plans that are 'District' and 'Locality' centres which do not have Executive City Councils. Thirdly, there is the Council of Ministers. The Government retains broader powers such as:

- organizing and operating the State Land Fund;
- defining the competencies of the provincial governments and of the ministries:
- creating totally and partially protected zones; and – deciding on the utilization of the beds of territorial waters and of the continental shelf.

g) Chapter VI. The Transfer of the Right of Use and Benefit

The most important principle is that which permits the transfer of the use and benefit of land by succession in favour of the spouse and heirs. It must again be mentioned that it is not the property itself that is transferred but the right to its use and benefit.

In addition to succession as a result of the death of a titleholder, the transfer of intra-structures, construction and other improvements attached to the ground is also permitted provided the licensing entity authorizes it. In this case the State may opt to acquire these improvements for itself. And precisely because it is not the land which is transferred, the *Land Law* determines that a new licence would be necessary for the new owner of the previously mentioned improvements. The only exception would be urban buildings where transfer of the building is effected with the right of use and benefit of the land.

h) Chapter VII. Termination of the Right to Use and Benefit

These are the forms of termination that need to be known: expiry at the time limit of the lease ('*prazo*') or of the renewal period; renunciation by the titleholder; revocation by the entity which conferred the right. In the latter case reasons must be given to justify the revocation, to guarantee that it will not be done arbitrarily. Only when sufficient cause is shown to exist, will there be revocation.

In some cases, revocation can be made subject to compensation, when it is done to further the interests of the State. In other cases, when it is done due to the non-implementation or non-completion of the plan for exploitation, there will be no provision for compensation. In all cases of termination of the right, the immovables incorporated into the land will be vested in favour of the State: that is, the immovables become the patrimony of the State.

i) Chapter VIII. The National Land Register

The National Land Register is the principal instrument that guides us in relation to the State Land Fund. The National Land Register organizes all the data that characterize each plot of land, in such a way that we can plan for the better utilization of land. The register provides the following information: first, the economic and legal situation of the land – signifying the state of usage and the rights exercised over it; secondly, the qualities of each zone of land – that is, the type of cultivation or usage favourable to each region; and, thirdly, all the statistical data necessary for the good usage of the land – the size or area of each occupied or unoccupied zone, the type of usage, the condition of fauna and flora, etc.

j) Chapters IX and X. Registration and Final Provisions
The Registration and Final Provisions set out the following:

i) The right to use and benefit conferred by means of a licence. After obtaining a licence the beneficiary must register it at the proper registry office.

ii) The most important principle intended to guarantee the observance of the *Land Law* and to protect the land as patrimony of the people is the requirement that all transactions that directly or indirectly violate the provisions of the *Land Law* will be considered null and void. That is to say, parties to such transactions will not be able to back their claims by claim of law. Moreover, if a business should cause harm to the State or to other citizens it may be reason for the payment of compensation or for the imposition of penalties, fines and imprisonment.

iii) At the moment on which all of the land, without exception, becomes the property of the State, the old owners cease to be owners of the land. In effect, the *Land Law* does not recognize any right to ownership of land. There are only users, as if they had never been the owners of the properties they used. Because of this the former owners will have a period of time in which to regularize their situation by obtaining the respective licences.

iv) It is within the power of the Ministry of Agriculture to clarify by published notice any doubts that may arise in the implementation of the *Land Law*. Nevertheless, it is best not to confuse doubt with questions that require regulation. In effect, the present law to a great extent depends on rules that still have to be published for each sector as, for example, with respect to agriculture, for industry, for transportation, public works, and the like.[3]

The Land Law and Revolution

In essence the principles of the *Land Law* elaborated above synthesized the experience of generations of poor and dispossessed Mozambicans in their struggle to regain the land. If the object of land law is normally to legitimate possession by conquest, the new Mozambican law set out to legitimate repossession by revolution. It aimed to give juridical coherence to the recuperation of usurped soil, to proclaim the restoration of usurped sovereignty, to affirm the revival of usurped dignity, and to consolidate the recapture of a usurped means of making a living. In its symbolic function, the law was like a flag of liberty that flew over soil reconquered, a soil that had been drenched with the blood and with the sweat of generations of slaves and forced labourers.

The land was doubly alienated under colonialism, not only in the sense that it was placed under foreign ownership, but in the sense that it became an instrument of pain and humiliation, the scene of back-breaking work for pitiful remuneration, a zone of punishment and control. To free the land and to free the people on it: this was the double objective of Frelimo from the moment of its foundation (1962). Where the Frelimo organization claims special merit for itself is in the way it transformed armed struggle for national independence into the people's revolutionary war (1964–74). More particularly, it takes pride in having clearly defined who the enemy was: not a nation, nor a people, even less a race, but a system. Thus the goal of the struggle was not to take over and Africanize or Mozambicanize the existing exploitative state – to replace one title owner with another – but to abolish it altogether and build a new society aimed at eliminating all forms of exploitation. In short, the objective was not to expel foreign exploiters so that local ones could take their place, but to get rid of all forms of exploitation.

This was vital to the policy developed on the land. The basic historical fact from which all legal relations flowed was that the land was nationalized. The new State came into being (1975) with the land belonging to the whole people through the State (Article 8 of the Constitution). This fundamental constitutional principle meant that any new *Land Law* had to be concerned essentially with the regulation of land use rather than with the determination of title.

The underlying principle of colonial land law was that ownership was crucial. The person who proved title to a piece of land and could do what he or she wanted with it, could use it, could neglect it, and probably could even abuse it, at will; he could sell it to whomever he pleased, mortgage it to raise funds, and lease it out to bring in rent. In some urban zones, concepts of overriding public interest made a faint appearance, but basically the owner was monarch of all he surveyed. He could even control its destiny after his death by appropriate testamentary dispositions.

The colonial authorities disposed of title at will, completely ignoring ancient rights of farming, pasturing and fruit-collecting. Family farmers were expelled without compensation or, alternatively, they were permitted to remain as servants and labourers on land which they and their fore-fathers had worked for generations; the traditional authorities became active agents in this process, offering themselves as recruiters of labour and collectors of taxes.

In the meantime, after the Liberation War started, contradictions began to appear within the ranks of the liberation fighters themselves. One of the issues involved the question of land use – one group within Frelimo favouring co-operative farming with the produce being made available for the collective war effort, another preferring private direction of labour and private control of the product. The decisive victory of the first group established the basis for land policy when independence was won. The experience of co-operative work in the liberated zones produced a consciousness and a method of organization that carried through into the independence period. Mozambique thus produced its own revolutionary 'model', based on its own revolutionary experience. The law that emerged was not an invention of idealists, but the expression of something already gained through hard experience.

In other African countries the option at the time of independence was seen as being between capitalist farming on privately-owned land for the market, on the one hand, and family subsistence farming on communally-owned land, use being allocated by traditional authorities, on the other. The outcome was usually a compromise in which certain zones of the country were reserved for one type of farming/ownership, others for another. Pluralist solutions were defended as being the most democratic and the most productive.

The Mozambican attitude was that such pluralism merely meant the co-existence of two types of exploitation, each equally undemocratic and oppressive: the colonial–capitalist type and the traditional–feudal type. Accordingly, Mozambique rejected both the manner in which the choice was defined and the solution that was offered. The Constitution declared that one of the principal objectives of the new society was the 'elimination of colonial and traditional structures of oppression and exploitation and the mentality that underlies them' (Article 4). This meant that neither the 'colonial–capitalist' nor the 'traditional–feudal' models could be carried on into the post-colonial state. In concrete terms, it meant the destruction of both colonial-type land law and of customary land law.

An important fact was that almost all the large farms had been abandoned by their owners in the transitional period before independence. Plantation owners and small colonists alike preferred to flee to Portugal or South Africa rather than become Mozambicans and identify themselves with the new society, as did a significant number of persons of Portuguese origin in other walks of life. In the wake of this flight, in order to pay the workers' salaries, to provide seed, to give emergency treatment to livestock, and to market produce, the State was compelled to intervene: it had to take over the farms. The most developed land therefore came under state control not by virtue of nationalization, but through abandonment and rescue. No formal confiscation was necessary or undertaken: the ownership disappeared with the owners and, in terms of the provisions of a general statute dealing with abandoned properties, the farms devolved to the State after a period of three months absenteeism.

The choice facing the authorities, therefore, was not whether or not to nationalize the large farms, but whether or not to denationalize them. As the *Land Law* indicates, the decision was firmly against any re-parcelling out of these large land-holdings; nor were there large investors waiting to take over. On the contrary, many abandoned small-holdings were consolidated into large state farms, or else made available to peasants living communally and working co-operatively on them.

At the same time, the traditional chiefs and headmen were being totally stripped of their political and legal powers. New political and legal institutions were established through the length and breadth of the country based on election and popular participation rather than on inheritance and age; these in turn resolved problems according to the revolutionary principles of the Constitution rather than the traditional principles of customary law.

The new *Land Law* took account not only of these historical facts, but of the economic fact that Mozambique is a large, potentially rich and vastly underpopulated country – depopulated by its history of slavery, deportation and emigration. Huge areas of fertile land lie uncultivated under forest – the problem is to clear the land, not to find it. Thus there is no shortage of land; but there is a shortage of people and skills. In this context, the basic strategy in the rural areas had been to encourage the dispersed households to come voluntarily together in communal villages based on co-operative living and co-operative production. These villages were regarded as the only viable means of realizing for the people their rights to education, health and knowledge as guaranteed to them in the Constitution; also, they were the only way of breaking with the immobilism and superstition of centuries, and of liberating the creative capacities of the working people.

At the time the *Land Law* was adopted, perhaps no more than ten percent of the peasantry lived in communal villages. Though the percentage may be small, the number of families involved runs into hundreds of thousands, all gaining experience which could serve for relatively rapid advances in the coming years; the communal village pattern is regarded as irreversible and the model for the future.

The great bulk of the rural population still live in scattered homesteads, occupying a large part of the land, eking out a bare living and producing a small surplus by growing food and livestock. This is an economically and socially important part of the population that constitutes the great majority of the Mozambican people, and produces a significant part of the food sent to feed the towns. They are regarded as having a historic right not simply to subsist on the land, but to use it as a means of creating wealth for the country and for themselves. Thus they farm the land which they occupy, as of right, without paying rent to the State and without being in any way answerable to the traditional authorities which are now abolished. The fundamental principle is that they farm on their own account without employing outside labour. Thus family production continues to exist on a large scale and obtains extensive protection from the law, subject to a policy of encouraging voluntary adherence to communal villages.

Finally, there still exists a relatively small but economically valuable group of private farmers who hire labour and produce for the market. Although their numbers are reduced, their legal rights and duties occupy a relatively large part of the new law. This should not cause surprise. The state farm sector is made up of public enterprises which operate largely in terms of government policy, according to internal regulations and the principles of public and administrative law. Though their existence needs to be affirmed in the *Land Law*, their operation need not be governed by it. Similarly, the co-operative sector is regulated by the general principles of co-operative law set out in a special law of co-operatives. As for the family sector, it is so vast and dispersed that even if it were believed correct to define and register title to use and benefit in each case – and this is not the policy – the necessary mechanisms simply would not exist. This leaves the privately-owned farms as the most problematic sector of all, the one that requires the most precise definition.

The *Land Law* looks at the continued operation of these private farms in the light of constitutional provisions on property rights. The Constitution recognizes four types of property: first, state property, such as the land and all apartment buildings, public enterprises, state farms and state enterprises; second, co-operative property, such as the co-operative field of a communal village, and property belonging to consumer co-operatives and artisans' co-operatives; third, personal property, such as clothing, furniture, a motor car or bicycle, tools of trade, a bank account, personal effects; and fourth, private property, such as a factory, a fleet of buses, an electricity-generating dam, a grocery shop, and a farm worked by hired labour; basically, this includes property in respect of which labour is employed to create profit for the owner.

The Constitution backs the consolidation and development of State and co-operative property while at the same time giving unqualified protection to personal property. Private property, on the other hand, is given grudging recognition. It is not defined. Further, the Constitution merely declares that private property is subject to obligations and cannot be used to the detriment of the objectives of the Constitution, foreign capital being authorized to operate within the framework of the state's economic policy. Since all the land belongs to the State, it is clear that farm land as such cannot be privately owned. In fact the new *Land Law* makes it clear that no private legal transactions in land are permitted. Land can neither be sold, nor mortgaged, nor hired out. It has ceased to be a commodity; like the sea and the air, it belongs to all.

If land cannot be sold, mortgaged or leased, if it loses its quality of alienability, if it ceases to be disposable by testament, what remains of property law? Property law is not abolished, but its character is drastically changed, and the whole nature of real rights is transformed. In the traditional–feudal society, land law is essentially an extension of family law; in capitalist society, land law is essentially an extension of the law of contract; in a socialist society, land law is essentially an extension of public law. What happens to real right, is that personal property becomes more important than private property, and movables become more important than immovables. The balance changes and the law is greatly simplified, since it is much easier to establish norms in respect of means of consumption – whose destiny it is to disappear in the course of their enjoyment – than to establish norms in respect of means of production, whose destiny it is to reproduce themselves. In particular, proof is greatly simplified: instead of an elaborate system of registered titles, reflecting a variety of hierarchically organized interests in the same (immovable) object, possession and a receipt usually suffice.

But then, how can there still be guaranteed rights in relation to the use of land? What protection does the private farmer have – whether foreign investor or local entrepreneur – against arbitrary deprivation? The basic solution is that private farmers operating within the overall economic plan have guaranteed leasehold rights for set periods formalized in registered licences given by the State. Provided they continue to farm in terms of their undertakings, they cannot be disturbed in their rights, whether they be a Mozambican miner returned from a neighbouring country with enough savings for a tractor, or a manager of a deteriorated tea or sugar plantation requiring extensive foreign investment, or a market-gardener operating on the outskirts of town.

This legislation is one more proof that the law is not silent amidst the revolution. On the contrary, it speaks in a different, louder voice than before, and to a much wider audience.

It has a real life for millions of people, even in its new form of regulating use rather than of determining ownership. Workers consult it when they wish to know how to set about regulating their rights to vegetable plots in the green belts; local government officials refer to it when mobilizing the people on the need for conservation, especially when applying special measures to prevent the burning of bush and forest as a means of clearing land; the judges in the people's tribunals apply its provisions in the resolution of disputes.

Two examples recorded during a visit to a people's tribunal in a rural area in the north of the country, illustrate the kind of case the *Land Law* has to deal with – not giant property transactions with batteries of lawyers and sheaves of documents and seals on both sides, but the problems of peasants in their daily lives, solved by the peasants themselves without professional legal aid. In the one case, a man about to leave to work in town had given a neighbour the right to work his lands for an annual fee. He had been away a few years and, on his return, asked to get the land back and the fees which had not been paid. The president of the court was barely literate, his four companions all illiterate. All of them were peasants in the area, dedicating one morning a week to the court to which they had been elected by their neighbours. The president told this author how the case had been resolved:

> We told the man that since the Revolution and in terms of the *Land Law*, land could no longer belong to someone who was not using it. This man had gone away to earn money elsewhere, and the one who had stayed behind to work for several years on the land was the one who could remain with the land, and, what was more, he did not have to pay for it.

The second case concerned a complaint by a member of the women's movement that one of the peasants in the area chased her and her companions off a salt pan allocated by the village assembly to their organization. The judges explained that they had told the man very firmly, first, that the women had the right to the use of the pan, and second, that even if he had a right to use the pan, the way to exercise it would not have been to abuse the women, but to have approached the court in the manner which the women had done.

The *Land Law*, like most new revolutionary laws in Mozambique today, is seen as consolidating the gains of the past, providing structures for the present and pointing the way to the future. Thus the *Law* has a strongly programmatic character, a feature of law in a revolutionary society. Understanding the distinction between law as a set of operative norms and law as a programme, is fundamental to any analysis of revolutionary law. The programmatic aspect is particularly pronounced in the early years of the revolutionary society. But it will always be there, because the materialization of each programme in terms of concrete political and legal rights creates the necessity for the elaboration of the next programme. The *Land Law* is programmatic in the sense that it educates, it lays down guidelines, and establishes a legislative contest in which future state action can take place. The wide language used, the broad categories, and the constant interaction between law and politics, are seen as virtues rather than defects. This is a stage of rapid destruction of the old and rapid construction of the new. It would be considered premature to attempt precise definitions at this moment, to lay down detailed legal provisions in relation to a practice that is still maturing. At present, it is believed, the law should establish the framework for development, and leave the formulation of more precise rules to the future. Thus it is contended that lack of technical rigour in the law is more than compensated for by popular participation in the processes of its drafting and implementation. The guarantee of its correct and effective application lies essentially in the extent to which it is comprehended and 'assumed' (taken over, internalized) by the people affected by it and not in a network of complex and supposedly watertight provisions understood by few except a handful of specialist lawyers and judges.

The new law may be solving the problem of the just use of the land, but it cannot solve the question of efficient use of the land. It cannot grow food nor conserve the soil, nor guarantee crop marketing. In institutional terms, it still has a markedly preliminary character, and as yet awaits the establishment of a national register. The process of promulgating the necessary regulations is a difficult one. The problem here – and one of the fundamental problems of the whole of 'popular justice' – is how one can simultaneously combat legalism and promote legality. Without precise norms meticulously applied, there is always the danger of arbitrariness and abuse of power. The President of Mozambique has, in the fulfilment of his duty to 'safeguard respect for the Constitution', frequently referred to very real abuses that have taken place and that weaken public respect for the revolution. At the same time, excessive formalism, worship of the letter of the law, and the autonomizing of legal relationships so that they lose their contact with the life of the people, also undermine public respect for the revolution. The process of promulgating the regulations necessary to give institutional form to the broad principles of the *Land Law* is, therefore, a difficult one, and will require much thought and attention to detail. These regulations will be essentially technical in character, and will lack the resonant language of the *Law* itself, defining the procedures necessary to achieve the purposes of the *Land Law*; at the same time, they will have to be comprehensible and relatively easy to apply.

Despite the lack of regulations, however, the new *Land Law* has already had its impact, and its principles are already being applied. The *Law* establishes a way of looking at the land; it gives coherence and legitimacy to new social and productive relationships. It is a bulwark against the past which might restore itself by stealth and inertia, and it takes its place alongside many other measures which in their totality represent a new kind of legality associated with a new kind of society. In the African context it offers wholly new solutions. Together with the revolutionary new family law project, it may be regarded as a landmark piece of legislation, one that completely alters the terms of debate in the law.

The argument of imposed law versus traditional law must be regarded as a false one in the light of revolutionary law. The basic themes of the new *Land Law* came from the peasantry themselves, at a time of intense struggle against both foreign domination and indigenous power structures. The *Land Law* emphasizes that the people do not simply inherit law, or submit to law imposed on them from outside. They create law, and become themselves the instruments for the implementation of the new norms which they have evolved. The new revolutionary law in fact has a clear relationship to both the old inherited law and the new imposed law; a relationship of *opposition*, of struggle against both. It defeats the old law as it defeated the old colonial power. And it is in the very process of struggle, of growing food during the war, of distributing the surplus, that the community's consciousness is created and the necessary personnel formed to carry through the changes.

Scholars need not be alarmed. Scholars still have a role, even if we acknowledge that the raw material of great ideas lies not in our heads, nor in our libraries, but in the activity and struggles of the people. Without becoming populist, without pretending to be what we are not, we can use our skills to record and generalize what has already been achieved. And those of us with experience in different continents have an especially useful function to perform, in encouraging the inter-flow of information and ideas across the boundaries of language and prejudice. It is not so much that we in Africa need to match up to the universities of the West by producing our own Americanists and Occidentalists, as that scholars in every part of the world should become sensitive to the great and universal issue of our day – exploitation and the struggle against it.

Conclusions

A number of conclusions may be drawn from the foregoing. First, the great choice facing the peoples of the Third World is not between submitting to legal forms and concepts imposed from outside on the one hand, and restoring indigenous or traditional forms on the other; nor is the problem to create an amalgam of the two, each with its own social or geographical sphere; the fundamental question is how to constitute new institutions and develop new concepts which will correspond to and serve the needs and interests of the people, and which are popular in form and popular in their mode of implementation.

Second, scientific legal thought has an important role to play in societies undergoing profound social transformations in the sense that it gives coherence and legitimacy to gains already made, helps to shape the institutions of the new popular sovereignty, assists in creating programmes for future development, and acts as an important instrument of social education.

Third, if different countries undergoing revolutionary change tend to adopt similar legal institutions, this is not because they are necessarily imitating each other, or transferring a 'model' from one society to another, but because similar problems and experiences necessitate similar solutions. In this sense, the essence of revolutionary law would be the same in all countries, independent of continent or the type of colonialism formerly experienced or the nature of the pre-colonial societies. At the same time, each revolutionary process has its own specifics, just as each person has his or her own personality. And these 'particularities' will have an important impact on the constitutional and legal forms which emerge.

Finally, lawyers need by no means be silent amid the roar of revolution. On the contrary, they have an important function to fulfil, not as opponents of change but as activists for progress, helping to clarify and apply the new norms in a way that facilitates the desired transformations, that eliminates arbitrariness and that defines in clear and understandable terms the rights and duties of citizens. In this context, technical aptness and the explicit revelation of the logic that underlies legal thought – in other words 'jurisprudence' – become valuable tools in the hands of the legal worker or law teacher concerned to make his or her contribution to the wider revolutionary process.

Notes

1. See generally, *Mozambique Land Law*, an official document translated under the auspices of the Committee on African Studies, Harvard University, with an introduction by Albie Sachs. This introduction is substantially reproduced in this article.
2. This section as well as section two are based on the author's understanding of the intent of the *Land Law* as gleaned from the text of the statute as well as a Government communique entitled *Official Explanatory Note*, both printed in Portuguese.
3. End of translation of the official text.

2. The Question of Access to the Courts*

The question of access of the people to the courts is a fundamental question, using the term access in its widest meaning. It is related to the question of simplifying the laws, to popularizing them and making them better understood, to the criteria for recruitment and training of the judges and lawyers in general. It is also related to the question of the functioning and procedure of the courts. In other words, the question goes far beyond the problems of providing proper legal aid.

In Mozambique our strategy has not been to replicate what existed before, as far as justice was concerned: that is, to have many judges, many lawyers, many public prosecutors, technically capable enough but inaccessible to the majority of the people for economic reasons and in any event serving the wrong policies, serving the interests of a minority; we have rejected the idea that it is good to have many codes, many laws, if they are incomprehensible to the majority and contrary to the interests of the people. In short, our objective has never been to Mozambicanize the pre-existing system, simply replacing those colonists who went away with local personnel. It follows that, in our view, the law should be subservient to the citizens and not to the lawyers. In turn, the lawyer's prime concern should be the placing of his knowledge and know-how at the service of the people, with the laws being his tools of trade and the defence of legality his constant objective.

In the framework of the principles already referred to and using the experience of justice in the liberated zones during the armed struggle for national liberation as a base, a new law on judicial organization was approved in December 1978. It created people's tribunals at each administrative level starting with the level of the locality, neighbourhood or communal village, then the level of the district, province and finally the Supreme People's Tribunal. In addition the new law provided for the office of State Procurator.

In the people's tribunal at the lowest level there are no professional judges; the judges are elected from among the local population on the basis of their common sense, feeling for justice and their knowledge of the revolutionary principles contained in the Constitution. They are persons who know the

* An earlier version of this paper by Gita Honwana Welch was given to the *Conference on Access to the Law*, Harare, Zimbabwe, 1984.

problems of that community; they know the people of that area, their procedures are open and flexible, and for that reason we state that the people's tribunals at this level are those to which the people have most access, where they are closest to the courts and get the best results. It is in fact these grassroots courts, the direct product of our revolutionary process, that act as the inspiration for the reconstruction of the legal system, to make it even more responsive to the interests of the people.

> The fact that they are free from the application of colonial laws and legalistic formalism enables the local people's tribunals to affirm the cultural values of the people as well as their feeling for justice. Thus, they become a source of inspiration for the creation of new law and for the functioning of the whole legal system. [*Report of the Frelimo Central Committee to the IVth Congress*, 1983].

In the people's tribunals at the lowest level all procedural formalism is reduced to the very minimum. Participation of the population is an important aspect of the functioning of the people's tribunal in general, but at this level its importance is doubled. In reality it is the population that, due to the fact that it has direct experience of the case which occurred in the community, serves as witness for the defence or prosecution and supplies valuable information to the court regarding the facts of the case, and helps it to reach a just decision. In these courts, although there is no formal presentation of the case, although there is no defence lawyer or public prosecutor, these functions are exercised by the participants. Normally, the trials are announced in advance and the people are invited to participate.

In the people's district and provincial tribunals, the formal procedural requirements are greater but whenever possible the court moves to the place where the incident in question took place. Thus, the participation of the population is very much easier than if they had to make the journey to the main town of the district or to the provinical capital.

At times we can say that these sessions of the court turn into real educational classes on our laws and the work of the courts. In addition, the courts at a district or provincial level work with elected judges, four per section (as well as one professional judge) who are chosen from the community, workers, peasants, members of what we call the democratic mass organizations, such as the Women's Movement, civil servants and other workers.

These elected judges play an extremely important role in the divulgation of our laws and in the resolution of specific questions raised in the courts. It has become common practice that in relation to certain questions in the ambit of family law the interested parties speak with the elected judges before putting the case before the court. Often there is a reconciliation by consensus and the problem is cleared up without having recourse to all the formalism and delays that a court case can represent.

Thus, access of the people to the courts is not simply another political slogan. It is a necessity. It corresponds to the present phase of growth and spread of justice in Mozambique. In very concrete terms popular involvement overcomes the deficiencies in the preparation of the cases, assures a proper defence for the accused, guarantees a complete and rounded quality to the evidence, and assures that in reality the people exercise their power in the field of justice and raise their civic awareness by so doing.

I can affirm from my own experience how beneficial it was for the courts to have access to the people.

During my five years as a judge of the Provincial People's Tribunal, I made several journeys from the court building in which I normally operated to conduct the trial at the scene of the event. The criterion for the journey in each case was a sense of the importance of situating ourselves in the atmosphere in which the events took place, discovering the level of consciousness and political awareness of the people involved, of getting to the root of the cultural questions underlying the case. In addition, the collaboration of the community can be vital in clearing up questions before the court; it can modify completely what can be deduced from the preparatory documents of the case especially when these are not as complete as they should be, which, unfortunately, is often the case. And this means simply that the margin of error in the trial, which in the courtroom can be enormous, is at the place of the event almost non-existent. Perhaps of even greater importance is the educational value of the trial which probes beyond the specifically legal question of personal guilt to engage with the population in serious dialogue about the bases of good and bad conduct. Let me give examples.

On one occasion I began a trial of a case in which four people were accused of attempted murder. They had begun to burn to death a woman. Though the facts of the case are fortunately unusual for my country, the underlying issue is still an important one. This tragic and nearly fatal event had taken place in a small, poor, isolated village on the frontier with South Africa, in an area relatively untouched by the revolutionary process. In terms of the old code still in force, it was clear to myself and the elected judges from a simple reading of the witnesses' statements that the accused, if the facts were proven, would merit an extremely severe sentence since it was clearly barbaric to try to burn someone to death, no matter what the reason. On the day of the trial three witnesses appeared; two others indicated that they could not come because, as those present explained, one of them was very old and for them to leave the place where they lived to go to the local administration to catch the transport for Maputo (where the People's Provincial Court in question was situated) would have required a walk for a whole day and a night. Anyway, we decided to carry on without the missing witnesses and the trial began. However, as the hearing proceeded, something came to our attention that had not been discernible from a simple reading of the files: the feeling of the defendants seemed to have mirrored the feeling of the whole community, namely, that the victim of the burning was a witch and as such should die for the benefit of the community. In the old tradition of that community witches ought to be burnt alive, not simply killed. The problem had a deeper dimension and it became clear to us as judges that it could not be treated simply as a criminal case detached from its underlying social reality.

On the basis of this feeling that there were important missing facts, we adjourned the hearing and decided to transfer the trial to the small locality of Catuane where the events had taken place. On the appointed day, we took with us the accused who were being held in Maputo jail, and after travelling along 30 km of tarmac road we drove along the track which leads to Catuane. It took a full hour to travel along the 30 km of track and by the time we arrived we were impatient with the difficulties of the terrain, the holes in the road and the discomfort of the journey. When we reached Catuane we found a crowd of around 100 people waiting for us. The court held its session under a tree in a clearing. We found out later that some of the people had walked nearly 50 km to be present at the trial. Many of the women were bare-breasted and some of the men were dressed only in a loin cloth. With the exception of one or two workers in the administration, no one could read or write. It was a rural community composed of peasants who led their lives still largely rooted in the only norms of conduct within their reach, the norms of traditional law, with its positive and negative aspects, with its spirit of social solidarity but also with its burden of deep obscurantism (superstition).

We heard the people, many more than those who had been indicated as witnesses in the files. Everyone had something to say. That community did not question the fact that there were witches. Witchcraft was part of their beliefs, their culture and mental outlook. This trial lasted, without break, the whole day. As the facts became clearer, the basis on which we should reach a correct evaluation of the accused's conduct also became clearer. We learned the importance of seeing our role as judges in the context of the ongoing process of the cultural transformation of the people. We learned the necessity to know the tradition of each district, each locality, each communal village of our country, to know the feeling of the population so that our action could produce the desired results. It is true that the court has a clear function which is to apply the law, but the law cannot be applied abstractly, and above all, as we are dealing with laws which we inherited from the past, and which are not completely adjusted to our reality, we have to apply them in a creative and flexible way without compromising the underlying principle.

During the trial an intense dialogue was established in which the members of the population explained at length to the court the life of that community and the events which had taken place. They affirmed their belief in witches and witch doctors, something which emerged clearly from the facts themselves. So we asked them how it was that the witches and witch doctors who, like all Mozambicans had also wanted national independence, had not been able to achieve it using their supernatural powers. The short silence that followed was a silence of realization, of the absorption of a new approach to the problem by the people.

Each of the accused was sentenced to a period in prison not exceeding one year given the exceptional extenuating circumstances. The work of defence counsel had been of great help, but even more important was the process of the trial itself, the active participation of the population who knew the case and who succeeded in transmitting to the court the real circumstances which had motivated the events. By their participation, the persons present and we ourselves had learnt something. Justice and the system of power which it represented was not something alien and distant from them; they too were involved in it and took responsibility for it.

We were aware that the trial had by no means banished superstition and obscurantism from the minds of the population. But the issue had been fairly and squarely posed for the people. And we, for our part, had succeeded in understanding a little the motivation of the defendants and the whole of that community; in appreciating the enormous social and economic under-development and the necessity of carrying out a profound process of political action; in seeing the need to raise the level of consciousness; and above all in giving the necessary priority to creating the conditions so that future generations would have the advantages of schools, and be themselves able to win the battle against obscurantism and ignorance using the weapon of scientific knowledge.

On another occasion we held a trial *in situ*, right in the heart of Maputo, on the workshop premises of a large firm which was an agency for the importation and repair of motor vehicles. The question was of one of fraud involving a large sum of money. This was at a time when the struggle against this particular type of crime was becoming intense and our state through these large and small frauds was being robbed of millions of *meticais*. Nearly 300 workers of the firm attended the trial which had the function not simply of punishing the guilty and acquitting the innocent, but of educating everyone present against fraud, whether large or small, and of showing those present our courts in action. The case was technically complex and depended to a considerable extent on accounting evidence. It was far more formal than the trial in Catuane had been, but nevertheless workers in their overalls came forward to testify before returning to the gallery of half-lubricated and semi-repaired cars in the large workshop. Work was suspended for several days as the trial proceeded, but the workers' organizations and the administration of the agency thought it well worthwhile because of its educational and 'consciousness-raising' value. These examples convey something of the way we see the problem of creating a genuine system of popular justice in Mozambique, of involving people in the process of justice so that they feel the system is theirs and take responsibility for it, so that their access may be that of participants and not of petitioners.

But however important the gains we have made on this front may be, they do not by any means eliminate the need to ensure that in concrete cases the individual accused or litigant has adequate defence and legal assistance. In fact, in the People's Republic of Mozambique the right to defence is regarded as a constitutional principle (Article 35).

Although private practice was abolished by one of the first laws published in Mozambique after independence, the defence and legal aid systems are not yet nearly as well organized as they should be. To understand why this is so, it is necessary to look at the function of defence of the citizen in the global context of people's justice and in turn to situate the question of the legal apparatus in the context of the larger problem of dealing with the state apparatus. We regard adequate legal defence as one of the fundamental pillars of the building of people's justice and socialist legality; for us, people's justice must assure the equality of the citizens before the law, and this necessarily involves the question of equality of access to legal representation. But we regard the question as being much deeper than the one of providing legal aid. In an unequal society, the legal structures more than any other represent inequality. If access to legal defence depends on the financial position of the citizen, those who have no money are obviously at a great disadvantage. Even if there are thousands of lawyers practising in a given society, this does not by itself ensure that each citizen has access to such lawyers; and even if the citizens have the necessary money to pay for the services of a legal representative or can draw on some fund to do so, the formalism of the law can be so intense, the language so inaccessible and the procedures so alienating, that what the citizens have is access to lawyers and not access to justice. The majority of the population still feels left out of the exercise. Finally, even well paid, brilliant lawyers cannot accomplish much if the legislation which they apply, directly or indirectly, proclaims inequality and serves the interests of a minority, whether such legislation be inherited from the past or be new. It is not enough just to have your day in court. The law itself must serve the interests of the people, defend their sovereignty, and protect the rights of the individual citizens against abuse.

In Mozambique after independence the number of professional legal workers dropped to near vanishing point as a result of the departure of lawyers who had come to Mozambique to make money and now were appalled by the arrival of majority government, especially when one of its first acts was to prohibit private legal practice.

The objective of the nationalization law was to ensure that justice was taken out of the market-place so that the right to have legal representation would no longer be dependent on one's personal fortune. In more general terms, it was related to a concept of popular justice in which lawyers and judges would no longer be a caste standing aloof from the people and conversing with themselves in a mysterious technical language which only they could understand. The tendency for the creation of a new indigenous elite, a new class of local exploiters, so noticeable in many other newly independent countries, had to be combated from the start. As President Machel put it: we had to 'kill the crocodile when it was small'. In any event, many lawyers and judges, who had been willing to give independence a chance provided it ensured good pickings for themselves, decided that after all they did not want to be Mozambicans, and so packed their briefcases and containers and left. In many ways, this was a blessing, and not a disguised one at that. The question was not one of origin but of option. Those who stayed have served the country and the ideals of justice well. The most important question was not that of technical expertise, even less so that of race: what mattered was the question of identifying with the goals of the new society. Technical expertise detached from such goals at best will create false problems, at worst will be used to undermine those goals. We attribute high value to technique, but only when it serves the interests of people in general, and is not a tool of exploitation and privilege.

In creating new legal technicians we had to start virtually from scratch. In the words of the first Minister of Justice, himself a former distinguished advocate, 'we had to look the question of justice straight in the eye'. It was then well understood that we had to approach the problem as one of urgency but without being unduly precipitate. And in addition to all the problems we had inherited from colonialism, we had to deal with effects of constant aggression, both in military and economic forms, and we also had to cope with the results of our own considerable inexperience, inadequacies and mistakes.

Thus, although we can claim substantial success in broad terms in ensuring that people really have access to a legal system that they really consider to be theirs, in the narrower field of creating a corpus of well qualified lawyers capable of offering legal expertise to the community – whether to individual or to large public enterprises – we have been less successful. The problem is not simply or even primarily one of quality, and by quality we mean the capacity to use their technical skills in a way that responds to the many and pressing legal problems thrown up by the revolutionary process itself. Although we find ourselves increasingly impatient with those who see slogan-mongering as a substitute for real work of high technical quality, we do not wish to produce a generation of supposedly neutral lawyers who stand apart from the great issues of the day. For this reason we see legal training as including an all-round preparation for facing the problems of our country, namely, the scourges of hunger, lack of clothing, illiteracy, superstition, ill-health, violent physical aggression and deliberate hoarding of scarce food supplies, and for dealing emphatically with any attempts that might be made to reintroduce tribalism, regionalism and racism into the country.

It is a process in which we all have participated, and one which never ends. The main problem is in reality ensuring that the great capacity the people have, when properly organized, of resolving matters in a just way, is reflected at all levels in the functioning of the legal system.

Against that background, we might look directly at the question of legal representation in the courts. As already explained, the very nature of the grassroots courts at the local level makes it inappropriate to have qualified lawyers participating in their proceedings. The access of the citizen there is direct and confident, as a direct participant in the process, so that professional intermediaries would only harm the process – certainly at this stage.

At the level of the district people's tribunal, in cases where there is a possibility of a jail sentence being imposed up to the limit of the court's jurisdiction (two years), the normal procedure is for someone working in the court to be appointed as official defender on an *ad hoc* basis. This is clearly not satisfactory, and represents the weakest area of legal aid in our court system.

In the provincial people's tribunals, on the other hand, legal defence is guaranteed in all criminal cases where there is the possibility of a jail sentence. Each provincial court has attached to it at least one public defender who has taken a special course administered by the ministry and whose function it is to defend the accused. In addition, in the case of more complex matters, we have a system whereby the judge can call upon legally qualified persons working in the public sector or even in the private economic sector to represent the accused in any particular trial. Normally the defence lawyer is the choice of the accused. In each tribunal the judge will have at his or her disposal a list of such persons and will attempt to get the services of whoever is most experienced in the field in question.

The public defenders receive a fixed salary, and the other lawyers continue to be paid by their ordinary employers. In addition they both normally receive an *ad hoc* emolument for each case fixed by the judge on the basis of their experience, the complexity of the case, the assiduity they have shown and the financial capacity of the accused. Though small in comparison with the vast fees commanded by private lawyers in other countries, these fees make a useful addition to the lawyers' salaries.

The position in civil cases is a little different, reflecting the great changes that have taken place in commerce and the vast reduction of commercial litigation since independence. The overwhelming majority of civil cases these days are concerned with family disputes, more particularly with divorce and with child support. In family matters, where the emphasis is on informal procedures, experienced court officials are generally the ones who help litigants prepare their documents and present their case. The list of qualified lawyers is always available to the judges in the case of more complicated matters.

To sum up, what scant resources we have are fairly distributed, the fundamental principle being one of need rather than of the financial resources of the litigant. However, a number of observations need to be made. First, there is the obvious gap of trained legal assistance at the level of the district people's tribunal. Second, the quality of the work of the public defenders needs constantly to be upgraded. It is not an easy thing to create a new style of advocacy. We know what we do not want: we do not want the old style of self-important lawyer looking for technical points with which to show off his or her cleverness, upset the opposition and unnecessarily complicate the case. Nor do we want subservient bureaucrats with the mentality of officials unable to imagine themselves in the position of the accused and unable to offer a vigorous defence. To achieve what we want, lawyers capable of offering lively defences within the context of the general goals as outlined in the Constitution, will still be a long process. Third, we need some form of legal organization to which citizens seeking legal advice can go, whether they be couples thinking about a divorce or someone wanting to open a restaurant or to farm a piece of land, to mention just a few of the activities where the law plays an important role. Fourth, we need to create a legal service available to embassies, international organizations and foreign investors capable of giving objective advice on questions of Mozambique law. In our country the inter-relation between the old codes and the new legislation is often quite complex; but even when we have succeeded in reformulating all the laws, simplifying them and making them more reflective of our social reality, we still believe that citizens and others have the right to good legal advice.

A start has been made in the right directions inasmuch as we have a draft statute prepared for a National Service of Legal Defence and Legal Aid. The path forward has been mapped, but we still have to take the first step.

At the more general level, too, the evolution of popular justice in our country, and with it the developing of the relationship of mutual access between the courts and the people, requires attention in a number of fields. The network of people's tribunals at the locality and district levels is far from complete. We are proud of what we have achieved in this field but parts of our population still live in areas where the new structures are not operative.

We have to re-organize and re-invigorate our whole system of legal training, concentrating primarily on courses for new judges, prosecutors and defence lawyers, but not forgetting the importance of training specialists for the economic field. In this respect, we need to break away from the traditional methods of selection of candidates for courses, give far less emphasis to formal qualifications and pay far more attention to modes of training appropriate to the surroundings in which the persons concerned will be working.

We have to push forward rapidly in the field of drafting new laws. Our objective is to do away completely with the whole system of colonial law which both in subject matter and in style does not correspond to the needs of our society. We have made considerable progress, starting with the Constitution, the fundamental law which acts as the foundation of all other laws. We have passed new legislation relating to land law, economic questions, private trade and made important alterations in the field of criminal law to make it more responsive to the concrete problems we face of violations of the rights of citizens and of the people as a whole. We already apply new principles in relation to family law, and have adopted nationalization statutes which have been important instruments in equalizing access to education, health, insurance and accommodation. However, the old Portuguese penal, civil and commercial codes are still operative in large areas of our law and their continued existence is an example of our difficulty in creating, in the short term, new legislation more suited both in form and content to our needs.

We need a new, complete and systematic set of laws that correspond to the new nature of our society, and although we believe that it is the people and not lawyers who make the law, we accept that good legal draftsmen have their role to play in helping the people achieve what they want.

Finally, we need urgently to transform the procedures of our courts, particularly in relation to criminal matters and particularly in the higher courts. Despite efforts at speeding up the process and making it less formalistic, we are still dominated by a cumbersome, excessively document-oriented procedure (and this is a society in which oral communication is still strong) which impedes the evolution of true popular justice.

3. Changing the Terms of the Debate: A Visit to a Popular Tribunal in Mozambique*

It was July 1979 and we were in a small village in northern Mozambique, 1,500 km. from the capital. In the background I could hear *vivas* being shouted and drums being beaten but my excitement was of another kind, the cool excitement of an English-trained legal empiricist about to discover facts, in this case not only facts, but virgin documentary facts. Because, right in front of me on the table in the shade of a large cashew tree, lay a big book with heavy binding, and in that book lay the first judgments of one of the first popular tribunals to be created in the first revolutionary country in southern Africa. I had already sat in on the lectures given at the Law Faculty to the young law students who were to constitute small brigades to start what was called the implantation of popular justice. I had heard from veterans of the armed struggle for national liberation how the basic principles of this system had evolved in the liberated zones even before independence; how popular justice meant justice that was popular in form, in that its language was open and accessible, popular in its functioning, in that its proceedings were based essentially on active community participation, and popular in its substance, in that judges drawn directly from the people were to give judgment in the interests of the people. I had attended a national conference on justice at which the brigades had reported back and had collectively analysed their experience as the basis for the new law on judicial organization; and now in this village I had met the new judges and seen that at least in its composition the court corresponded to the injunction that it be popular: all five members were farmers or workers in the village, two were female, and one was young, barely twenty.

But the true test of popular justice lay not simply in its appearance, in the fact that it was being conducted by barefoot judges in the shade of a cashew tree, nor even in the logical and political coherence of the principles that underlay its foundation. It depended on the concrete ways in which it set about solving the concrete problems of the people, and this was what I was about to discover. What would the book reveal – something really new, or something, as Professor

* This paper was originally presented by Albie Sachs to the *Conference on Traditional African Law in Situations of Change*, Lisbon, 1984, and published in the *Journal of African Law*, London, Vol. 28, Nos. 1 and 2, 1984.

Allott might have put it, that was simply the old customary law with a few revolutionary trimmings?

> On the 21st January 1979, [the first decided matrimonial case read] a husband (name given) asked for repayment by his wife of 300 escudos (about US$10.00 at the time). On the following day his wife asked for a divorce. The man asked why. She replied, 'because I am tired of you, you are a polygamist and have treated me badly. When you asked me for the money I answered: if you want the money you will have to take me to court.' That was why he went to the court. But the judges decided that she had every right to ask for a divorce, since she felt herself liberated as a Mozambican woman who did not want to be exploited. The money has been given to her for her use, and did not have to be repaid. The couple were separated, and the man went to his other wife.

There were many more cases of a similar kind, written in the large handwriting of someone not used to handling a pen. I copied them all down, and already it was clear to me on a factual level that in at least one court in one village the principles of popular justice were working.

It might seem that, apart from the references to the liberation of women, the case was a simple one, even banal, which would have been decided in much the same way by any fair-minded judge anywhere in the world. But that is exactly the point. If the principles argued for by the supporters of legal pluralism had been followed, the determination would have proceeded on quite different lines, according to different criteria producing different results.

The first question in that zone would have been whether the parties were Muslims. If so, polygamy would have been recognized, and the woman would not have been able to get a divorce, even though she would not have been ordered to repay the money which her husband claimed.

If they had been Catholics, and this the man's first wife, the marriage (if properly celebrated) would have been indissoluble, and the second 'marriage' would have been null.

Alternatively, if they had been identified as members of 'tribe' A, which followed the principles of patrilinearity, the wife could only have got a divorce if her parents paid back the *lobolo* (marriage consideration). On the other hand, if they had belonged to 'tribe' B, which was matrilineal, the wife could not easily have expelled her husband, but if he chose to live with another woman, he would leave behind all the household goods with his first wife. In any event, in these two cases the judges would probably have declared that a polygamous marriage existed and that the wife would have to learn to live with her husband and his other wife.

Finally, if the couple had been classified as 'civilized' in terms of their lifestyle, the court might have decided to apply the civil law to their situation, and have found that since they were not legally married, there was no marriage to dissolve, and that if the money had been given to the woman as a loan and not as a gift, she would have had to pay it back.

If there had been full-fledged legal pluralism, there would even have been separate courts, with a Muslim judicial council for Muslims, a canonical court for Catholics, or a court of the chief or elders, depending on the ethnic group of the parties, if they were identified as belonging to group A or B. (I deal only with the simple situation where both parties are identified with the same personal law. The possibilities and problems of choice of law multiply if, say, the husband is a Muslim belonging to ethnic group A, and his wife a Christian belonging to group B.)

It is clear, however, that questions of ethnic origin or religious belief played no part in the determination of the case. The existence of a marriage was taken for granted as a matter of common knowledge, and the way the marriage had been constituted was regarded as irrelevant to the matter of how the parties' rights and duties were to be construed.

The first question that arises is: how was the transformation from pluralist to unitary principles and practices accomplished? The fundamental problem, the central drama of any revolutionary process, is that the system must be changed while the people remain the same; there is a discontinuity of institutions coupled with a continuity of the people. The people must change themselves.

In the case of the evolution of the system of popular justice, the necessary transformation depended on three factors. In the first place, the basic message about the need for national unity, about the people exercising new forms of power, was conveyed by Mozambicans to Mozambicans. It was not brought by missionaries from outside attempting to impose their vision of the world on the people, not even by local legal missionaries returned from 'advanced' law schools abroad. Indeed, the legal missionaries of today tend to carry exactly the opposite message, urging the people to conserve their honest customs and avoid the heathenish ways of the West. One cannot help thinking that in this respect alone it was as well that the judges were largely illiterate, otherwise they might have learnt from the latest science of the West that what they were doing as a matter of routine was theoretically quite impossible.

In the second place, the new values were applied by members of the community chosen by members of the community, and not by outsiders. Furthermore, they were being applied by representatives of the community as a whole, and not by one section against another; by women as well as men, by young people as well as old. Whereas in traditional society generation judged generation and gender judged gender, here it was the *povo* (the people) judging the people.

Third, the transformation in the justice sector accompanied and reinforced other transformations, and reflected a new sense of justice related to general changes in the lives of the people. Not only was there the dramatic transformation from the humiliation of colonial domination to the new sense of freedom that came with independence, there were major changes in material and social life – people moved from dispersed family homesteads to life in a village, from scratching a precarious living from the soil to working as basket-makers in a co-operative, from existing in a world at the mercy of the elements to life in a community with a school and health post.

Since examining the records mentioned above, we have had the opportunity to look at the records of scores of the six hundred or so popular tribunals which presently exist at the local level in different parts of Mozambique, and also to sit in on trials in various parts of the country. On the basis of information so gained, we can say with confidence that, in general terms, popular justice in Mozambique is popular, it is just, and it exists as an extensively verifiable fact.

The second part of this paper deals with two questions that arise: one, granted that the system has verifiable existence, what were the circumstances that made its 'implantation' possible in Mozambique? Two, does its emergence mean that the question of having a unitary system of justice in a country with a multiplex culture is finally resolved?

The Evolution of Popular Justice

It is important to determine the specific circumstances which facilitated the evolution of popular justice in Mozambique both so as to avoid the temptation to extrapolate this experience unjustifiably to other countries with different processes of development, and so as to be aware of the limits of the achievements thus far accomplished. The basic fact is that popular justice was not the invention of progressive lawyers determined to renovate an out-of-date legal system, nor was it a copy of legal systems that existed in other countries that may have shared similar political philosophies in a general sense. It was an integral part of a much wider process of social transformation inside Mozambique itself that had started with the proclamation of a general insurrection against colonial domination, that included the whole long period of armed struggle for national liberation, took in a series of practical experiences in the liberated zones where the very necessities of consolidating a new type of government in areas from which both the colonial and the traditional authorities had fled, had forced the rapid evolution of new types of judicial structures; and finally had been associated with the rapid institutional transformations experienced in all spheres and in all parts of the country immediately after independence.

Of particular importance was the rapidity and profundity of the destruction of what in Mozambique was called traditional–feudal power. This was a process very specific to Mozambique, where it may be said that traditional power had become so closely identified with colonial power that, when the latter was destroyed, the former collapsed with it.

The underdeveloped nature of Portuguese colonialism forced it to adopt a high degree of direct state compulsion in its quest for labour, and the chiefs and *indunas* were given important though junior tasks in the structures of compulsion. They helped in the recruitment of forced labour and imposed severe physical punishments on those they regarded as recalcitrant; they participated in the collection of taxes, the provision of information to the authorities about resistance, and in the recruitment of police and soldiers.

Those chiefs who showed signs of patriotism were summarily dealt with, many ending their lives as a result of torture, starvation or execution on the prison island of Ibo, not far from the village mentioned in the opening section of this paper. Thus to the degree that the chiefs exercised power in colonial times, they lost their popular authority; even the judicial power they exercised became tainted, since it was regarded as a perk for the services rendered to the colonial state, handsomely rewarded in terms of the gifts necessary to 'open' the court. The fierceness of class struggle in the countryside just before and just after independence remains as yet largely unrecorded. Suffice to say that in interviews with the new judges, a strongly expressed theme that emerges is the contrast they seek to establish in their work with the venality of the justice administered in the past by the *regulos* (chiefs); in their view, the only custom that really counted in the courts of the chiefs in the late colonial period was the custom of visiting the chief's house the night before the hearing with a gift more extravagant than that given by the opponent. It might be worth observing here that, in counterpoint to the lively debate occasioned by the remark from the chair by Professor Richard Abel to the effect that the legal profession in Africa might have had a material interest in promoting a single court system functioning on the basis of a unified and codified set of laws, a large class of chiefs and religious leaders also existed with an equally strong economic stake in maintaining separate norms of which they would remain the natural and well-paid custodians.

The destruction of the institution of traditional power was accompanied in the post-colonial period by the creating of new organs of local power, in which active parts were played by women from the women's organization and by young people from the youth organization; the courts were accordingly not the first institutions to break away from the gerontocratic and sexist assumptions of traditional society, imposing, as it were, new values from the top. This was a period in which the working poor were asserting themselves in every sphere of society, politically, socially and culturally.

The complex interaction between law and mode of production in the rural areas as referred to in other papers would accordingly seem to require considerable refinement as a result of the experience of popular justice based on the rural poor in Mozambique, where new norms serving community interests as defined in a new way are consciously adopted and serve to accompany and facilitate changes in the mode of production rather than merely to reflect them. (It is not the scientist who discovers the connections hidden behind the forms; the 'forms' are overtly adopted by the people in a deliberate attempt to alter the reality of their lives.)

At the technical level new juridical solutions had to be found to correspond to the new ways in which justice was being administered. As so often happens in situations of rapid change, new institutions preceded and shaped new norms. The extended use of the *de facto* union as the central figure in family law emerged from the practice of the local popular tribunals rather than arrived as the fruit of legal thought in the far-away capital. Without going into details, it may be mentioned here that the records of the popular tribunal of Maiaria played an important part at a certain stage in the discussions of the evolution of the draft new family code, of which key sections have already been adopted by the courts. The *de facto* union moves from the margins of the law of marriage to become its most important figure, and thereby the great bulk of the population whose marriages have not been registered are brought within the jurisdiction of the state courts. The near universal applicability in practice of the concept of the *de facto* union is facilitated by the fact that, behind the multiplicity of ways in which families are constituted, family problems are roughly the same. There is unfortunately a uniformity to matrimonial misery in broken-down marriages, which has nothing to do with whether the parties were married by Muslim or Christian rites, according to *lobolo* or in the civil registry, or with whether they are small farmers in Cabo Delgado or office workers in Maputo, or, indeed, with whether they are living in Manhattan or London or Moscow or Maputo.

Alcoholism, wife abuse, financial anxiety, sterility, sexual problems, incompatibility of temperament and interests, these are practical questions giving rise to practical problems requiring practical solutions. As far as the court is concerned, it matters not at all whether a wife-beater is Muslim or Christian or was married by *lobolo*; what he is doing is wrong and unlawful, and his wife is entitled to appropriate protection from the court.

The Problem of a Unitary Legal System

If one accepts that the popular justice system is in fact operative and does in large measure succeed in accomplishing its stated objectives, does this mean that the problem of having a unitary legal system in a country of great cultural diversity has been solved?

The answer clearly must be no. To begin with, the area of operation of the system has been geographically uneven, coinciding basically with zones of greatest population concentration and being strongest in areas where new forms of community organization are most present. There are large parts of the country where at the local level the popular justice system is still remote, both in the physical and the political sense. But even in the areas where the system is operating and operating well, great difficulties remain. These are the difficulties found in any legal system anywhere in the world, but especially acute in a society of great cultural diversity undergoing rapid transformation.

The undoubted successes of the popular justice system by no means do away with the problems of unity in diversity – they merely alter the terms of the debate. What the debate ceases to be about is whether to have 'a western legal system with customary law trimmings, or a customary law system with western trimmings, or some fusion of them both', as Professor Allott has argued. This is not just because the term 'western' is too limiting to a country like Mozambique, which is happy to draw on the experience of 'eastern' countries, whether socialist or not, as well as from the rich and original experiences of the Latin American world. It is because the debate in his terms is considered a false one. If aspects of traditional law are rejected, that will be because they are regarded as feudal, as impediments to the creative capacity of the Mozambican people, and not because they are African. Similarly, if the objective is eventually to eliminate completely the Portuguese legal codes, this is not because the codes came from Europe, but because in their language, content and assumptions they are inconsistent with the legal needs of the Mozambican people. The family contemplated in the section on family law in the civil code simply bears no relation to the Mozambican family; the whole section in the code on property rights loses its meaning once the land is nationalized; the nature of commercial activity has changed so much that the commercial code becomes increasingly ineffective, and so on.

The debate, then, is on how to create new laws that reflect the new Mozambican personality and express the interests of the Mozambican people as a whole, on how to involve the people in the legislative process, and on how to ensure that they are involved in the implementation and control of the law that emerges. These are the fundamental questions: not 'African' versus 'western'.

Furthermore, the debate ceases to revolve around technical questions such as codification or re-statement or judicial control of customary law or no control at all. The question of sources and internal choice of law also becomes obsolete. In fact, in the context of the practice of the popular tribunals, it is difficult even to convey to Mozambican lawyers and students what the debate about internal conflict of laws is all about, let alone propose solutions; people have become quite used to the fact that, in their dealings with state institutions, ethnicity is not a relevant factor, and that church and state are truly separated.

But closing one debate simply opens another. The problems of relating the unified set of norms to a population with a diverse culture still exist, but express themselves in different forms. Basically they amount to finding the correct strategies so as to relate what might be called a vast sector of informal popular justice, with all its improvisations, heterogeneity and conservatism, to the more dynamic, coherent and progressive popular justice system of the courts.

Law may be seen as operating in five dimensions: as principles, strategies, institutions, procedures and norms. In the case of family law, we have seen that in Mozambique the constitutional principles of uniformity, laicity and equality are followed through and materialized at the institutional, procedural and normative levels and given shape by the unitary system of popular justice. But this does not answer the critical question of how the law deals with customs that imply different principles or that were formerly enforced by means of other institutions, procedures and norms. It is here that the question of strategies becomes all important. In any society law basically operates through three strategies, with a variety of intermediary possibilities: it may penalize defined behaviour, reward it or ignore it. The key question is always to find the appropriate strategy in relation to any specific phenomenon at any specific time. There are many aspects of traditional law which continue to influence the behaviour of certain sections of the people and which are regarded as retrogressive, such as child marriages and polygamy; similarly there are others which are regarded as having strong negative features, such as the way traditional marriages have been turned into commercial transactions. What strategies should be adopted towards them?

The fundamental legal strategy adopted towards these negative phenomena has not been that of repression, but that of deliberate ignorance. This is not the same as tolerance or even neutrality in the sense that the customs are in fact combated by the state. But the combat is restricted to the political, educational and cultural sphere, and takes the form of moral persuasion and not of legal compulsion. Ignorance by the law means that no one can base a claim, say for restitution of cattle, on the existence or failure of *lobolo*. At the same time, no one can be punished for demanding or paying *lobolo*, even if in grossly excessive and exploitative amounts. In looking at any particular family situation, the law as law simply ignores the existence or otherwise of *lobolo*. This strategy has the advantage of flexibility, since if historical circumstances were to change, the agency of the law could be invoked, either to give limited recognition to *lobolo* or to impose penalties for its practice. At the moment of writing, an extensive national discussion on *lobolo* and related institutions is reaching its closing stages – more than half a million persons have attended meetings throughout the country organized by the Women's Organization to discuss the question – and changes in legislation could well come about, possibly resulting in a limited recognition of *lobolo*.

Thus the state does not coercively impose its cultural values on the people, but strives by means of education and example to bring about changes.

Social institutions operating outside the formal legal system still play a significant role in resolving family questions in line with their own philosophies. The family is regarded as a major social institution and the basic cell of the new society. The great majority of family problems are still solved within the context of the family itself, and here there is no reason why the parties should not follow traditional customs if that is their wish. Similarly, believers are fully at liberty to turn to their religious institutions for help, and if they prefer to solve their disputes applying the norms of their faith, there is no one to stop them from doing so; Catholics can continue in their daily lives to apply the canonic law and Muslims the sharia. The only limitation is that any arrangement arrived at will not in itself have legal effect, though its practical results may be recognized by the law. And the only prohibition – though there is no express legislation on the subject – is that no recourse may be had to the traditional ethnic structures such as the chiefs' courts, since this raises questions not so much of cultural values as of the exercise of power.

Thus, in practice, the courts will be invoked only when all other social institutions have failed and at least one of the parties wishes to submit the matter to popular justice. In Pemba, for example, an area of strong Muslim influence, we were informed by one of the local Muslim leaders that matrimonial disputes are normally heard first by the family council, and if this fails to achieve a settlement, the matter comes to him, and if he fails to find a solution, he advises the parties to go to the local popular tribunal, with which he has excellent relations. A typical case, he mentioned, would be one where the parties agree on a separation, but not on who should stay on in the house.

That the courts are accepted by the people is proved by the volume of business that is voluntarily brought to them. In all areas where the new courts have been established, there appears to have been a constant stream of people submitting their cases to popular justice. A feature of the system is the extent to which it is being used by female litigants, acting in their own right and not through husbands, uncles or brothers. From one point of view, family law at the local level is the law of women's rights, since men have such power through custom and through their economic and physical strength as not to need the law on their side, while women can only succeed if the organized power of the community comes to their aid. But the records show that a significant proportion of cases are initiated by men who wish to arrange their family affairs in a way which the community to which they belong, as represented by the judges, will regard as correct.

The new popular tribunals thus become much more than places where individual disputes can be settled in a dignified and a fair way. They become instruments of public education, zones of struggle between old ideas and new in which the new always have the advantage, though they do not always triumph. The people are the teachers and the taught, the element of continuity in the process of change. In this way, the question of the future of traditional law moves from the elegant rooms of the Museum of Ethnology, in which we have been so comfortably housed for the duration of this interesting conference, and begs to pose itself a new problem requiring a new methodology in the more spartan quarters of the Museum of the Revolution.

4. Transforming Family Law: New Directions in Mozambique*

Introduction

Traditional law is the system of rules formerly applied by the traditional courts, whether of the chiefs or religious leaders. It still influences to a greater or lesser extent the behaviour of large sections of Mozambican people. It is not, however, used as a formal source of law in the state courts of independent Mozambique. A study of the operation of more than 600 local courts, dozens of district courts, ten provincial courts and the appeal court shows that the emerging legal system, based on the principles of what is called popular justice, draws extensively on certain aspects of traditional law without incorporating its rules into its normative system.

The popular courts do not recognize different systems of family law for different groups. Race, place of birth, ethnic origin, religion, social occupation, style of life, degree of 'civilization' or 'assimilation', to use the tests that have been or are still applied elsewhere in the continent, are irrelevant in determining the rights and duties of parties. There are no chiefs' courts or religious courts, only a single state court system operating in terms of the uniform principles of popular justice. There is no system of internal conflict of laws to decide which personal law is applicable in a particular situation, because there is only one system of law for all, what is regarded as a Mozambican law for Mozambican citizens, rather than a law of tribes, religious groups, races or social classes.

The Constitution of the People's Republic of Mozambique, adopted by acclamation by the Central Committee of Frelimo a few weeks before independence on 25 June 1975, declares unequivocally that:

> citizens . . . enjoy the same rights and are subject to the same duties independently of their colour, race, sex, ethnic origin, place of birth, religion, education, social position or occupation. [Art. 26]

It adds that all acts designed to prejudice social harmony or create division or situations of privilege on the basis of colour, race, sex, ethnic origin and so on

* This article first appeared as 'Transforming the Foundations of Family Law in the Course of the Mozambican Revolution' in the *Journal of Southern African Studies*, Vol. 12, No. 1, October 1985, and was later reprinted in Alice Armstrong (ed.) *Women in Law in Southern Africa*, Harare, Zimbabwe Publishing House, 1987.

are punishable by law. Whereas other independence constitutions with similar equal rights clauses add a proviso excepting traditional family law and land use, the Mozambican constitution permits no exceptions, and in fact contains a provision to the effect that one of the fundamental objectives of the People's Republic of Mozambique is to 'eliminate the colonial and traditional structures of oppression and their corresponding mentalities' [Art. 4].

A pointer as to what are to be regarded as oppressive traditional structures can be found in the many constitutional articles dealing with relations between men and women. The principle of equal rights must guide all legislative and executive action [Art. 29] and it is explicitly declared that 'the liberation of women is one of the essential tasks of the State'. Furthermore, 'women are equal to men in terms of rights and duties, such equality extending to political, economic, social and cultural spheres' [Art. 17]. Finally, to complete the constitutional picture in this respect, the section on the functions of the judiciary declares that 'the Supreme People's Tribunal shall guarantee the uniform application of the law by all the courts in the interests of the Mozambican people' [Art. 72].

This paper sets out to answer two questions that will immediately spring to mind: first, how is it possible to have a unified system of family law in a country characterized by such a diversity of family life? Second, even if it is established that traditional law is not a judicially operative set of norms and as such lacks formal legal significance, what is its social and political meaning for the Mozambican people today?

Before setting out to answer these questions, we would like to explain our use of the term 'traditional law' in preference to the more widely used phrases 'uses and customs', 'local uses' and 'customary law'. We reject the terms 'uses and customs' or 'local uses' because of their colonialist implications – we are talking about coherent normative systems applied by the courts of traditional society in a consistent and effective way. Therefore, it seems to us just as appropriate to call them the 'law' as it would be inappropriate to refer to the statutes of Westminster as the 'uses and customs' of the English.

At the same time we prefer the adjective 'traditional' to the more widely used 'customary' because of the context in which we employ the term: we feel that in the circumstances of contemporary Mozambique it is more useful to locate the system historically and sociologically than merely to regard it in formal terms as a source of law. We accept that in other countries where the legal rules of traditionally organized society are still operative in the courts, either with a sphere of their own or as aids to the interpretation of statutes, it might be convenient to refer to 'customary law', thereby distinguishing it from legislation. But where its significance is historical and cultural rather than purely legal, it would be misleading to use the term 'customary law' to describe this body of rules and procedures. In its day it was 'the law', just as in its day colonial legislation was 'the law'. 'The law' today is not conceived of as a fusion or amalgam of these two sources, but as something new being created through the system of popular assemblies and popular tribunals. If customary law, in the sense of rules of conduct, is still operative in Mozambique today, it relates more to issues such as the functioning of co-operatives, the use of food supply cards, the management of communal villages and the activities of the Women's Movement, than to the furnishing of bride-wealth.

For these reasons, when we refer to traditional law we mean the bodies of rules which were formerly applied by the traditional courts – whether of the chiefs or of the religious leaders – and which still influence the behaviour of large sections of the population to a greater or lesser degree, even though they are not recognized and accordingly not applied in the state courts of independent Mozambique.

The bulk of the material on which this paper is based was gathered by students and staff of the Eduardo Mondlane University during their so-called July Activities in 1979 and 1981. With the help of the Ministry of Justice, brigades of students and staff visited all the provinces of the country (except Niassa) during the July vacation. They collected information about traditional law, especially as it related to the family. Moving from the provincial capitals to selected districts and localities, they interviewed members of the Frelimo party and the democratic mass organizations, such as the Women's Movement and the Youth Movement, as well as officials in the Registry, judges of the people's tribunals, representatives of religious communities and individual citizens, both in organized groups and selected at random. In addition, information was culled from the Marriage Registries, while judgements of local people's tribunals were copied out in full. A principle objective of the enquiry was to get information on the processes whereby families were constituted and dissolved in the different parts of Mozambique, so as to enable a classification to be made of the country's different marriage systems.

The Diversity of the Mozambican Family

A notable feature of the information collected by the brigades was its diversity. Thus in the single province of Nampula it is possible to find no less than five major systems of marriage existing side by side: the traditional matrilineal system, the traditional patrilineal system (*lobolo*), the Islamic system, Christian marriages and civil marriages. Each of these systems has its own ceremonies and each creates its own patterns of family relations. It is not unusual to find the same couple married according to at least three of the systems, nor to find all the systems co-existing in the same area.

The traditional matrilineal system

The marriage system most widely adopted in the provinces of Zambezia, Nampula and Tete is the so-called matrilineal one in which for purposes of rights, duties and succession, the family line is traced through the mother. Normally such a family will be matrilocal, that is, when a marriage takes place, the woman stays on in the homestead or locality of her parents, while the man leaves his parental home to live in the homestead of the family of his bride. Though the position of the bride will be much stronger than in a patrilineal society, it would be quite incorrect to suggest that these are matriarchal as well as matrilineal societies. Women do not rule in matrilineal societies. A woman's children belong to the female line and frequently adopt the surname of the mother, but it is not she who exercises parental power so much as her uncles, brothers or cousins. Thus, although she is the key link in establishing intergenerational relations, the persons who exercise a dominant role both in respect of internal relationships and in respect of relations between her family and the world at large, are her male kin.

Many anthropologists claim that matrilineality is a characteristic of agricultural societies, in which the family field acts as the main source of family wealth, while patrilineality is a characteristic of pastoral societies in which cattle constitute the primary source of wealth. In general this pattern may be observed in Mozambique, but it is necessary to avoid undue schematicism, because it is possible to find social groups with the same productive base having different marriage systems. Thus the inhabitants of the southern coastal regions tend to adopt patrilineal marriage systems, while those further to the north prefer matrilineal ones, even though all practise the same kind of economic activity, namely fishing, supplemented by field crops and fruit. It may well be that in certain zones a dominant form of marriage system emerges, related essentially to whether or not the economy permits accumulation. As Dr Shula Marks suggests, the switch to patrilineality comes where there is accumulation, which cattle make possible in agrarian societies; the question is more one of transmission of property than of the type of economic activity.

In the matrilineal societies, where women are undoubtedly more protected *vis-à-vis* their husbands if not *vis-à-vis* their brothers, *lobolo* does not exist. Money changes hands, but in a purely symbolical way. Thus in the District of Magoe in Tete Province, the young man proposes marriage by paying the girl or her aunt or grandmother the symbolical sum of twenty-five *meticais* (less than one US dollar). If he gets half back, he knows he has been accepted. If all is returned, he has been rejected. After the marriage has been agreed on, the groom moves to the household of the bride's family where for a relatively extensive period of time he is obliged to perform services such as building a house, opening a field and contributing with game and fish to the family pot. Only after complying with these obligations may he and his wife and children move out to establish a new household, usually not far away from that of the wife's family. Should there be a divorce, it is he who leaves the home to return to his family, while his wife, the children, the home and the fields remain within the sphere of his wife's family.

This system, however, is undergoing considerable change. Nowadays it is not unusual for the groom to offer the bride's family a sum in cash so as to free himself of the need to render services, relegating his stay in their household to one of mere formality. In Zambezia the same term, '*pette*' which formerly referred only to services performed by the son-in-law in favour of his wife's family has now been extended to cover the payment of *lobolo*. This development is looked upon with great disfavour by the older generation who see it as yet another example of the degeneration produced by 'the appearance of money'.

The patrilineal system

In the south of Mozambique and in certain parts of the north, the traditional marriage system is patrilineal, that is, the family line is traced through the father rather than the mother. Normally this system is patrilocal in that it is the woman who leaves her family group to live with and 'belong to' the family of her husband.

The practice is an old and well-established one, and the term *lobolo* is used in all parts of the country to refer to any form of economic advantage that accrues to the bride's parents as a result of the daughter's marriage. Formerly paid largely in cattle, the *lobolo* given to the bride's parents served to compensate them for the labour expended on their daughter's upbringing and for loss of her productive and reproductive capacity. In addition, the *lobolo* was a symbol which concretized the relations being established between two families; the transfer of *lobolo* from one family to another created extremely solid bonds between the two families, while at the same time the *lobolo* obtained from the marriage of a daughter could be used to 'acquire' another woman for the brother, the cousin, at times even for the father himself. According to informants in Gaza and Inhambane, *lobolo* served additionally to stabilize relations between the new couple, since the wife would not lightly run away from her husband knowing that her family would as a result be obliged to restore the *lobolo*. It is clear, then, from the vast amount of testimony available, that *lobolo* has a great number of meanings and cannot simply be reduced to the phrase 'purchase of a woman' or 'bride-price', however central and concrete this aspect may in reality be by virtue of the fact that by paying *lobolo* the husband becomes the 'owner' (this is the expression commonly used) of his wife and of the children she bears.

In the region south of the River Save where migrant labour to the South African mines started, *lobolo* came to be paid in cash (at times in bars of gold) reaching ever higher amounts. The changes that migrant labour wrought in this zone have been fully analysed elsewhere: for our purposes, it should be pointed out that in Gaza and Inhambane provinces the normal age for a man to marry was no longer determined by the rites of initiation but by his first visit to 'Jone' (Johannesburg).

The traditional Muslim system

In the provinces of Cabo Delgado and Niassa, in a part of Nampula and in the coastal areas of Zambezia, Sofala and Inhambane, popular culture in all its aspects, including marriage systems, is profoundly influenced by Islam. The people in these areas have developed their own norms with regard to the establishment and dissolution of family unions, the manner of resolving disputes, and the way of distributing property after death. Muslims marry according to a ceremony called 'Nika', in the presence of a Sheik or other community leader. Polygamy is permitted to the extent of four wives (some say up to seven). The interviewees firmly denied that any *lobolo* was paid, insisting that at most a present called 'mahari', consisting of money or valuable ornaments, would be given to the bride during the ceremony. Unlike *lobolo*, '*mahari*' belonged exclusively to the woman as a sort of dowry given her by her husband at the time of marriage, and in the event of divorce, she was not obliged to hand it back.

Marriages according to Christian rites

The tenets of the Christian religion, both in its Catholic and its Protestant versions, continue to exercise considerable influence in many parts of the country in relation to the way families are constituted, even though, for a variety of reasons, the number of Christian marriages appears to have dropped substantially since independence. Generally speaking, the marriage officers of the different denominations insist that the couple first celebrate their marriage in the Civil Registry before marrying in church. The result of this is to ensure that in certain rural zones where Christian influence is strong there is a higher than average incidence of registered marriages (for example, in the agricultural areas of Angonia, where the church has many members, the rate of registration of civil marriages is much higher than in the nearby and apparently more 'modern' town of Tete).

Certain representatives of the Christian church said in their interviews that they were concerned about the decline in the number of church marriages, declaring that people were turning more to traditional ceremonies or merely setting up joint homes without any formalities, and doing so not only in Mozambique but in all of Africa. As far as their general attitude towards traditional law was concerned, these representatives tended to distinguish between polygamy and divorce on the one hand, which they regarded as evils to be firmly combated, and *lobolo* and the traditional ceremonies which preceded or followed marriage on the other, which they looked at with a more tolerant eye. Thus in the case of thrice-married couples (according to the civil law, Christian rites and traditional law) any problems that might arise would first go to the family council, then to the relevant church structures, and only if no solution could be found would they be taken by one or other of the parties to court.

As is well known, the principal characteristics of a Christian marriage are monogamy and, in the case of Catholic marriages, indissolubility. In the eyes of members of the church, the marriage derives its efficacy from vows made in front of the altar, on which the priest or minister confers a sacramental character.

The civil marriage

The university brigades paid special attention to the annual variations in the number of marriages registered in the Civil Registry. The results of their investigations suggested that after a small rise in the period immediately after independence, the number of registered marriages began to drop quite sharply, so that probably less than ten per cent of all new unions are registered today. Each year, relatively few people who marry see any advantage in registering their marriage. Most people marry intending to have a monogamous marriage, like that contemplated by the civil law, and have no legal impediment to their marriage such as age, existing marriage or consanguinity. In spite of this, registration seems only to complicate their lives without conferring any corresponding benefits.

New family relationships in the communal villages

The research data unfortunately contains relatively little material on the position of families in the communal villages. These villages have been set up voluntarily by peasants in a variety of forms and at a variety of times, and between them have a total population of over a million, constituting more than ten per cent of all inhabitants of the countryside. Such information as we have, however, suggests strongly that the higher the degree of political mobilization and the greater the extent of co-operative production in these villages, the deeper the acceptance of new values in the socio-cultural spheres. In Nampula, for example, it is in the more solidly established communal villages that the principles of the Constitution and the orientations of the party Frelimo have in general been the most strongly accepted. In these villages, polygamy is an increasingly rare phenomenon, and there is a constant increase in the percentage of marriages (whether registered or not) based on the wishes of the couple rather than on the determination of the families. 'Today our children go to school and get to know each other there; then they wait for each other with a view to marrying one day', said a woman peasant, member of the communal village 25th September, in the District of Meconia.

But there have been problems, especially in the early days. Women in Nampula were reluctant to leave their traditional family villages where, according to the matrilineal system, they could count on a degree of protection from their kinsfolk. To move to a communal village implied entering a mononuclear relationship with their husbands, without a guarantee of their lives being improved. It happened, for example, that some men left their original wives and children behind and entered into new 'monogamous' marriages in the communal village. However, the integration of men and women into co-operative production is transforming the nature of the family. In particular, polygamy loses its material base as family production gives way to collective production. In their new capacity as paid workers, women develop a new consciousness as well as acquire a new level of dignity in the family. Serious matrimonial conflicts are submitted to the dynamizing group or the people's tribunal and are resolved according to a system of values in which the fundamental principles of equality between men and women and protection of the rights of the child are respected.

A Unified Legal System

Conventional wisdom, based on the not always happy experience of other African countries, would suggest that in the face of such diversity of marriage systems, the only feasible solution would be to give equal legal recognition to each system, either through recognizing a personal law in an integrated state court system (as in Tanzania), or through having traditional courts for family matters operating side by side with state courts (as in Malawi). The criticism would be that, even acknowledging the value of a uniform legal system in promoting national unity, to impose the norms of one section of the population on the rest would be undemocratic. In any event it would be counter-productive in that it would promote national conflict rather than national unity: the uniform law would at best be a paper decree not really touching the lives of the people, who would continue making and dissolving their families in their diverse ways, simply disregarding the law. A similar argument, but put on a more materialist basis, would be that the problem presented thus far as one of cultural diversity is really one of uneven economic development. Without first transforming the economic base, especially in the countryside, any attempt to change radically the cultural and legal superstructure would be doomed to failure. To leap over stages of development sets back rather than advances the revolutionary process, and enables all the most conservative and reactionary elements in society to gain popular support by posing as the true defenders of the people's culture. At the ideological level, voluntarism and adventurism are to be condemned as reflecting the impatience of a *petit–bourgeoisie* that seeks to make massive leaps forward by force-marching the people, rather than advancing steadily with the aid of a scientific plan that takes into account the experiences of other countries at a similar stage in their development.

These are serious arguments that must be treated on their merits, even if at times they have been advanced opportunistically by persons wishing to protect feudal-type privileges (usually male domination) under a progressive charade, or paternalistically by those who have difficulty in crediting the peoples of Africa with the capacity for revolutionary transformation. In fact, as will be shown, the successful functioning of a uniform judicial structure applying a uniform set of legal norms depends to a large extent on a flexible and non-coercive relationship between the formal and the informal sectors of justice. Furthermore, the concept of process, of protracted struggle, is regarded as fundamental in ensuring the correct interaction between the new and the old, between the formal and the informal. Also, the objective is never seen to be that of destroying the old, but of transforming it, of developing the aspects that are positive and eliminating the aspects that are negative. Finally, the policy is to ensure as far as possible that the people should be at the centre of the process, so that the rate of advance in creating new structures is conditioned by the capacity of the people to assume new values. Though exhortation and mobilization have their role, the main way in which people alter their consciousness is by doing, by practice, and nowhere is this more evident than in the process of building up the popular justice system.

With these preliminary observations in mind, we proceed to the question: how is it possible to have a uniform court system applying a uniform set of rules to families constituted according to a multiplicity of different systems?

The first matter to be noted is that at the substantive level, behind the multiplicity of forms which the Mozambique family may take, there are strong points of identity both in the character of the family and in the nature of the problems arising, which facilitate the attribution of a single set of rights and duties to all. Thus virtually all Mozambican marriages have a popular or community character. There is community interest and involvement, quite independently of whether the couple are married in a church or a mosque or at the Family Palace (Civil Registry) or simply by payment of *lobolo*. The public recognition of the marriage comes from the fact that the persons live together as a family unit, more than from the rites and ceremonies that preceded or accompanied their co-habitation.

At the same time, the problems which give rise to family conflict tend to be the same independently of how the family was constituted: men abandoning their wives, excessive drinking, physical abuse, sexual problems, financial stress, sterility, incompatibility of temperaments and so on. These are practical problems requiring practical solutions, and there is no reason why the courts should not use the same basic criteria for their resolution, irrespective of whether the union was celebrated according to one set of rites or another. This really is the fundamental factor: the courts ignore the background cultural and religious circumstances, which are rarely relevant to the actual matter in dispute, and examine the issue in a concrete way as the problem of this or that household at the time of the marriage breakdown. The 'orientations' which the judges receive on how to deal with family disputes constitute principles equally applicable to all unions, whatever the background of the parties: that is, facilitate departure of a wife from a polygamous union; try to reconcile the parties where possible, but, where the breakdown is serious, grant a divorce on equitable terms that recognize the interests of the children; treat men and women as equal.

The religious, ethnic or cultural background might have a certain indirect evidential value, but will not be a factor in deciding on what norms to apply. The norms are these 'orientations' whose concrete application allows for some reference to local sentiment with regard to questions of timing and detail, but not to the extent of allowing religious or ethnic law to restore itself under the guise of 'common sense'. A wife-beater is a wife-beater, and it does not matter whether he paid *lobolo*, or is a Christian or a Muslim or a non-believer: if he makes life intolerable for his spouse, she is entitled to the protection of the court, and if the simple justice of the case demands that he be the one to be expelled from the home, since it is easier for him to build a new house than for her, so be it, whatever traditional law might have said. A preliminary survey of the actual practice of the courts at the local level in virtually all parts of Mozambique indicates that the largely illiterate judges achieve as a matter of routine practice what highly qualified 'Africanist' scholars have difficulty even conceiving of: roughly similar solutions are found to roughly similar factual situations of family stress throughout the country (or, as they say, 'from the Rovuma to the Maputo').

The substantive equality of family misery, independently of how the family was created, makes it possible to establish a hold-all legal concept that gives the courts a general jurisdiction to deal with all problems of family breakdown. This is an adapted and elaborated version of the *de facto* union, which in the conditions of Mozambique moves from the fringes of family law to its centre. With only ten per cent of marriages being registered, the remaining 90 per cent are largely regarded as *de facto* unions which for a great variety of legal purposes, especially in relation to the competence of the court, are equated to registered marriages. In practice the courts at the local level refer to the parties as 'husband' and 'wife' simply on the basis of social acceptance and without paying regard to the payment of *lobolo* or the performance of certain religous rites. This, then, is the practical strategy which the law adopts in relation to *lobolo*, religious ceremonies and other rites associated with traditional marriage. The law neither recognizes nor penalizes these practices. It simply disregards them for the purposes of finding the appropriate legal rules in any situation, subsuming them with all their particularity into the bland general figure of the *de facto* union.

There is no attempt to penalize practices regarded as wholly incorrect, such as polygamy and child marriages, nor practices regarded as having certain harmful features, such as *lobolo* and rites of initiation. But at the same time, legal rights and duties cannot be based on the rites and ceremonies associated with these institutions. In all parts of the country, independently of what was permitted by local tradition, the judges will regard it as wrong for a man to take a second wife. He will not be punished for so doing, but his first wife will have a judicial remedy if she chooses, and any determination in divorce proceedings made about the division of property or the custody of children would not be influenced by any claim he might make or imply to the effect that his religion or ethnic background permitted polygamy. Similarly, there is no legal prohibition on the payment of cattle by way of *lobolo*, but, as at the time of writing – when a great national consultation on the family is taking place, involving meetings organized by the Women's Movement and attended by a total of more than half a million persons – no one can go to court to argue that cattle so promised have not been paid, or cattle so paid should be restored.

At the same time, there is nothing to prevent persons from constituting and dissolving their families according to their religious beliefs or traditional ideas. Families may make their own arrangements without going to the Registry or the court: Catholics may regard their marriages as indissoluble; Muslims may marry and divorce according to the Koran; people may continue to follow the patrilineal or matrilineal family arrangements of their forefathers. The State does not interfere. It does not recognize, but it tolerates. The court does not intervene on its own initiative, but only when one of the parties invokes its aid. Then the court will apply the uniform state norms as already indicated. In many areas it is not unusual for the religious authorities themselves to send difficult cases to the courts. In Pemba, for example, Muslim leaders pointed out that family disputes first go to the family council made up of close relatives of the parties. If no settlement is arrived at, they go the Muslim judicial structures, and if these fail, it is the imams themselves who will refer the matter to the people's tribunals.

To summarize thus far: at the substantive level, the objective of family law is to give practical solutions to practical problems; at the technical level, firstly, a broad definition is given of *de facto* unions, secondly, the penal law is not used to outlaw traditional practices and thirdly, people are free to submit their family disputes to family councils and religious bodies if they so wish; the courts only act when their intervention is sought by one or both of the parties.

What is not permitted is recourse to what are called the 'traditional feudal' political and judicial structures associated with the chiefs and indunas. This brings us to the institutional dimension of the problem. The destruction of the power and structures of the chiefs, a process which started in the liberated zones and then was extended to the whole of the country, constituted the institutional pre-condition for the abolition of traditional law as an operative system. It was the colonialists who destroyed the real authority of the traditional structures by executing or deporting all the patriotic chiefs, and converting the rest into minor and corrupt agents of the colonial regime. These latter chiefs recruited forced labour, collected taxes, acted as informers and lined their pockets at the expense of the people. Hence their removal from power was warmly greeted by the population; recently elected judges in Pemba spoke bitterly about the corrupt behaviour of the tribally based judicial authorities in colonial times, declaring that of all the 'uses and customs' to which these chiefs were supposed to adhere, the most important one was the custom of visiting the chief's house on the night before the trial accompanied by a goat or a chicken or a large tin of cashew nuts. The relative ease with which the people accepted the destruction of the colonially-recognized tribal and religious judicial structures suggests not only that these structures were heavily compromised by their collaboration with colonialism, but also that the tenacious adherence to traditional structures and law widely commented on elsewhere might have had as much to do with the desire of a class of well-placed elders to protect their power, privilege and economic benefits, as with the desire of the people as a whole to defend their culture.

The destruction of traditional feudal power in Mozambique was accompanied by the establishment of what are referred to as the institutions of people's power. Concretely, this took the form of a rapidly established network of dynamizing groups, amongst whose functions was the resolution at the local level of 'social problems'. At a later stage, the 'implantation' of people's tribunals began throughout the country. *The Courts Act of 1978*, based on experience in the liberated zones and taking much of its detail from pilot schemes organized by justice brigades operating in all the provinces, opened the way to the creation by election of people's tribunals at the level of the locality and the district, and to the transformation of the already existing courts at the higher level. In the following seven years, something like 5,000 persons were elected to perform judicial functions. The bulk of them are poor peasant farmers, chosen in their community for their integrity and good sense.

A typical local people's court will have five members and two alternates, of whom at least one and usually two will be women active in the Women's Movement, and one will be a youth who has shown good qualities in his or her work in the Youth Movement. They will use the local language in their trials, making a short summary in Portuguese for their records (with the assistance of a local teacher if none of the judges can write). At the district and provincial levels, the elected judges who sit with the appointed judges are mostly workers, but other strata are also represented, and there will always be a fair number of women in their ranks. The research done during the July Activities coupled with direct experience which the authors have of the functioning of the tribunals, suggests that the new courts have been well accepted by the people, that in general they function well and provide effective solutions to the very large number of cases brought to them, and that they accomplish their task without applying the principles of traditional law.

The substantive technical and institutional transformations referred to above are taking place in the context of extensive socio-economic and cultural change. In the long run, the rapidity with which the new legal concepts take hold and become internalized as the values of the whole population, depends on the speed and depth of socio-economic transformations, especially in the countryside. In the meanwhile, changes in modes of production and changes in the cultural and legal superstructure proceed simultaneously, if not always evenly, each supporting and reinforcing the other. In concrete terms, this means that the new court system and the new norms of family law are most deeply rooted in the areas where new relations of production and new forms of social organization are most evident, namely in the communal villages in the countryside, and in the more strongly organized residential areas in the towns.

The current significance of traditional law

Although destroyed as a formal source of law, traditional law lives on in three fundamental respects.

First, many key aspects of the processes of traditional law have been taken over, transformed and integrated into the new system of popular justice, which owes much of its vitality and personality to this revolutionized inheritance. Traditional law always had a profoundly democratic character in that its norms were generally known by the whole population while its procedures encouraged extensive popular participation. It is not accidental that today a large number of illiterate judges, acting without legal codes, are able to settle disputes in a rapid, just and dignified way. They have behind them generations of experience in how to solve questions through the application of collective wisdom according to rational criteria. They call upon a culture in which questions are resolved through discussion and analysis, after having been looked at in a multi-faceted way and not according to dry legal definitions, and in which authority is exercised with tact and an attempt wherever possible to re-integrate the defaulter into the community. The success of the popular justice system owes as much to the continuation of the popular and democratic aspects of the traditional legal system (its procedure) as it does to the destruction of the latter's feudal aspects (its structure and norms).

The new laws which are being applied also represent a continuation of the popular or democratic aspects of traditional law in that they are couched in terminology as far as possible understood by the people and only adopted after extensive popular debate on their terms. The laws therefore do not seem to be the product of lawyers existing in another world; the law-makers are not so different from the judges and the judges not so different from those who come before the court.

Second, traditional law in all its complexity and detail, forms an important part of the cultural patrimony of the Mozambican people. Even those aspects regarded as negative need to be studied in their social and historical context if they are to be effectively dealt with. But in general the people have the right to know, understand and appreciate the society that their forefathers lived in, even if they are seeking to transform that society radically. A scientific and objective study of the past, freed from the distortions and defamations of colonialist ethnographers (as well as from the romantic mythologizing of some contemporary Africanists) is regarded as an essential part of the recuperation of the history and personality of the Mozambican people.

Finally, even though they may not be incorporated into the formal legal structure, there are a vast number of practices associated with traditional law which are either positive in themselves or at least not socially harmful or retrograde. They give vitality to social life and possess considerable meaning for the people themselves. The intricate and delicate procedures of *lobolo*, if shorn of their associations with the commercialization of women, continue to dignify the marriage process and to encourage inter-family solidarity. These practices live on as part of the culture of the people, as part of a diversity which, in the context of the process of change, enriches and strengthens national unity. Traditional law lives, but in a transformed way, as part of the people's culture and part of the unified system of popular justice.

Appendix A: Extracts from the Basic Record of a Local People's Tribunal[1]

This was a large book, with the first few pages filled in with the large handwriting of someone not used to writing often. Many words were written phonetically, there was no reference to legislation, no formal or complicated language. Yet the basic record of the people's tribunal of the communal village of Maiaria, about 40 kilometres south of Pemba, was clear enough.[2] The reader could immediately grasp the essence of the case, the evidence given and the solutions arrived at. About two thirds of the cases dealt with family problems, and what follows is a small selection of these.

1. The man who wanted his money back[3]

Case no. 4. On 21.1.79 a husband[4] asked for restitution of 300 *escudos*[5] from his wife. On the following day his wife asked for a divorce. The man asked why. She replied, because I am tired of you, you are a polygamist and have treated me badly. When you asked me for the money I told you: Why don't you go to Court? That was why he went to the Court. But the judges decided she had every right to ask for a divorce, since she felt herself liberated as a Mozambican woman who did not want to be exploited. The money had been given to her for use, and did not have to be repaid. The couple were separated, and the man went to his other wife.

2. The woman who refused to obey

Case no. 6 – 9.1.79. The man wanted to send his wife away because she did not listen to his orders. She went out with other men and would not say who they were. The woman replied: her husband was not interested in her because she had a child at breast, also, he wanted to marry another woman, also, he always drank, and when he was drunk he accused her of going out with other men, which was not the truth. The Court decides: the man must leave the other woman. At that time he was a *sipaio*.[6] But in 1978 he organized a third wife for himself. I asked him about this, and he said he could marry whoever he wished. After that he kept quiet, but got tired of me and stopped coming to my house. I'm tired of all these problems. The Court: this man must divorce this woman, he cannot have three wives, because in Mozambique and in this village we do not permit polygamy. But the man has two children, and he has to make a house for them, and pay $2,000.00 for materials. Every month he must bring them part of his earnings; if he fails to do so, the Court will send his wife to his work-place to receive the money there.

3. The man who got a second wife

Case no. 13 – 6.2.78. The husband left his wife and married another woman. The Tribunal: how can you abandon your wife and marry another woman when you know that in this revolution a man should not do this without a justified reason? The Man: I only wanted to get married. The Tribunal: you've got children, who will look after them? The second wife was called and asked how she could marry a man already married. She replied that he had told her he was not married. Certain '*responsibles*'[7] of the village said this was not the first time she had done this, nor the second, it was the third. The Tribunal decided that she had to do 20 days community service in the village centre, and the man 60 days, and that they had to leave each other alone.[8]

4. The wife who slept with the physical education officer

Case no. 15 – 7.2.79. The man complains that his wife has been sleeping with the chief physical education officer for the district. The latter denied this completely, but the woman said it was true. The Tribunal said this situation could not go on, she had to stay with her husband. But the husband decided: All right, we will divorce you, because it was a second wife, a polygamous marriage. They accepted this and they separated.

5. The man who discovered he had a certain disease

Case no. 17. The man complained that his wife was going out with other men. He discovered this as a result of a disease he caught from her which caused him pain when he urinated. The woman said, yes, it was true, she had had sexual relations with a man she had met in the street, whose name she did not know. The judges criticized her as a whore, and the '*responsibles*' as being undisciplined, since this was not the first time she had done this, nor the second, nor the third. They ordered a divorce according to the request of the husband, and told the woman that there was nothing for her to do but find the man with whom she had had sexual relations.

6. The husband and wife who had ceased to love each other

Case no. 25 – 20.4.79. A comrade[9] asked to be divorced from her husband because they had ceased to love or look at each other, and she did not like him any more. The man replied, not saying very much, that one night when he was sleeping after dinner, she suddenly woke him up, and said: Listen, my husband, I don't love you anymore, I only want to leave you. She then went to the '*responsibles*' of the area, who told her that their policy was to fight against divorce. Then she went to the Tribunal. The judges ask: As '*responsibles*' of the village, we are required to combat divorce, and here we are asked to grant a divorce. This is not the first time she asks, nor the second, nor the third. Ever since 1975 she has been asking for a divorce. Because we are alone,[10] we will refer the case to the district tribunal.

(Note: In the meeting with the university July Brigade, the secretary of the tribunal raised this case and asked the representative of the Procurator's Officer for his opinion. The latter's 'orientation' was that the court should wherever possible try to reconcile the parties, giving them a week to think the matter over.[11] If the problem was serious – as in the present case – they should grant a divorce. This was in respect of non-registered marriages. Registered marriages had to be referred to the district court.)

Appendix B: Justice that Kills in Order to Spread the Faith and Empire

John Bila's experience of the law in colonial times

'At that time in 1944 I was a cleaner-cook in the home of Mr Doctor Judge Moreira da Fonseca': Thus spoke John Bila, 63 years old, born in Chibuto in the southern Province of Gaza, presently resident in the Island of Mozambique, one thousand kilometres north near the mainland in the centre of the country.

The history which he recounts is the history of his past life, as well as the history of the lives of thousands of Mozambicans, a history that is at times simple, almost banal; at times complex, extraordinary, unbelievable. Nevertheless, it is a history that is true and a history lived through by a whole people. Thus, though we spoke to one individual, we feel it was a collective interview, and that the author's rights in relation to the story he narrated to us belong to the whole Mozambican people.

> At that time it was up to the master to want or not to want something. It was his will that counted, he could do whatever he liked to a domestic servant. When he wished, he could complain about us to the police and we would receive the *palmatoria* [that is, be beaten on the hands and all over the body with a heavy plank with a rounded end full of holes]. When we got to

the police, we weren't even called upon to speak, we only counted the number of strokes singing against our flesh, without even knowing what we had done wrong.

In January 1944, when I was 24, I was locked up in prison. No one ever told me why. Later we heard that a new police chief had arrived in the city, one Silva Pereira, who told the Governor that he was going to clean up Lourenço Marques [as Maputo was then called] because it was full of criminals.

I worked for a Judge, I was no criminal. To this very day I don't know why I was picked up. And we were many . . .

Extracts from colonial legislation

Regulations dealing with Native Servants. Document no. 5565 of 12 June 1944:

Preamble:

The growing influx of natives to the urban centres in search of work has created social problems the resolution of which requires rigorous control in these centres, not only to prevent wherever possible vagrancy and associated crime, but also to correct the bad conduct of domestic servants and other workers in relation to how they carry out their work.

Art.1. All male natives over the age of 14 who are permanently or temporarily resident in the [municipalities] of Lourenco Marques and Beira must be registered with the police in their local areas.

Para. 1. On registration, such residents will receive a document called the Service Book.

Para. 2. The above provisions shall be applicable to native women over the age of 14 . . .

Art. 10. Natives who work in the localities referred to shall be classified as:

a) Domestic servants;
b) Servants/employees of the State;
c) Servants/employees of private firms;
d) Carriers;
e) Artisans;
f) Ambulatory buyers and sellers . . .

Art. 25. Every Master shall, in relation to his servant:

. . . 7. Present to the police or order the presentation to the police, of any servant whom he intends to dismiss on the grounds of grave lack of respect, disobedience or refusal to work . . .

. . . 9. Not give benefits or allowances in cash in amounts greater than a quarter of the monthly salary.

Art. 26. Every servant shall, in relation to his master:

1) Obey orders . . .
3) Look after the goods of the master . . .
4) Make good any loss or damage resultant from malice, neglect or carelessness, by means of indemnity;
5) Have maximum respect for the master;
8) Not demand increase in salary during the currency of the contract . . .
13) Not give shelter in the master's house to any strange natives . . .

Art. 30. Violations by natives of the regulations shall be punishable by 15 to 120 days corrective labour.

Art. 44. Any native in the areas referred to in Article 1 who, through bad behaviour becomes an undesirable element or dangerous to public order and safety, shall be placed under the disposal of the Government for purposes of banishment . . .

Art. 46. It is expressly forbidden for natives to pass through the streets of the areas mentioned in Article 1 after 9 in the evening.

Our beatings were by the hour, not according to the crime.

On the voyage to the Island, on the boat *Colonial*, we were thirty, all bound to each other. We journeyed like cattle.

Each one of us had been surprised at work. There was not a criminal amongst us. Yet even when we went to the toilet, we had guns trained on us.

I spent ten years in the Island fortress. They told me that that was what had been decided at my 'trial' in Maputo. We really took a hammering. On occasions they beat us three times a day. As I said, they hit us by the hour, not according to the crime.

My regime was prison with hard labour. We had metal irons that joined our two feet, with a bracelet on each foot. In order to protect our tendons from being cut, we tied a piece of rope to the bracelets and pulled them up from time to time.

We were fed on flour, often rotten and without any gravy. Sometimes when they knew that officers were visiting the fortress, they gave us rice.

We worked outside all day long and returned to the prison at four in the afternoon. Just to secretly get a little bit of dried fish, we had to bribe the foreman, who was black.

In 1954 the Chairman of the Council of the Island, Rosa Cabral, decided to tar all the main roads. We worked on them, with chains on our legs. We built houses, fountains and streets. This was forced labour on top of prison and banishment. Others worked with us who were not prisoners.

Government notice no. 4963 of December 1942. Regulations concerning native labour contributions: Art. 1. All able-bodied native men between 18 and 55 years of age, are liable for accumulated labour contribution (service) for the purposes of public works in their collective interests . . .

Art. 5. Labour contribution refers only to five days service each year . . .

Art. 6. The following are considered public works of collective interest for natives:

1. Construction, repair, conservation of and planting of trees on streets;
2. Opening, construction and conservation of wells, springs, signposts, fountains and cattle drinking troughs;
3. Construction, conservation and cleaning of native villages and native locations (neighbourhoods) . . .
4. The clearing of trees and the opening of water trenches.

In the fortress they killed people for everything and for nothing – the punishments were horrible. Many people died of whipping, of beating with the *palmatoria* stick, of kicks.

They invented punishments such as the following: a certain Captain Barroso ordered us once to dig and dig next to the gates of the fortress until we encountered the entrance to a tunnel which, he said, linked the island to the mainland. The tunnel was supposed to have been a stone one made in the First World War. We dug night and day but never found a thing.

On another occasion, a certain commander Joaquim Bernardo ordered us to dig a hole and take out all the salt water and to carry on until we came to fresh water. The fresh water never appeared, but we dug for four weeks. This was in 1948, and all we found was arrows and old weapons from the time of the war of the Namarrais. They took all these arms in boats to Lisbon.

But the normal punishment was breaking stones.

Statement by fisherman Boia, 54 years old, resident on the Island of Mozambique:

As long ago as 1947, I remember seeing people breaking stones in this neighbourhood. The stone would be sold to persons from Portugal or Goa or other light-skinned people who came to the Island. Until 1957 there was a law that said that natives were not allowed to build houses of stone, only Portuguese and people from Goa and other foreigners could do so.

The stone was sold at three or five *escudos* a metre – it depended on the stone – the price could reach ten *escudos* [a very small sum]. The breaking was done by 'native servants' and by prisoners. The servants were trapped into this sort of work by means of taxes and forced labour. Women too were pulled into this work.

The cistern in front of the police headquarters on the island was built with stone by prisoners in chains. In the [poor] area of Esteo [in which the people live in reed constructions] a lot of stone went out. Whoever didn't pay taxes had to chop stone. Many died while breaking stone [so that the colonialists could have stone houses].

Decree no. 5076 of 20 March 1943.
1. Any natives who have not paid taxes for any years up to the present must pay off the shortfall by means of corrective labour, in terms of the law currently in force.

Notice no. 4768 of 27 June 1942.
Preamble: Unify and bring up to date laws dealing with native taxation – the most important source of income in the colony.

End the hut tax and give the native tax a personal character.

Create as well a reduced native tax (for unmarried women, divorced women and widows).

Art. 1. All natives of both sexes between the ages of 18 and 60 shall be obliged to pay the Native Tax.

Art. 5. The Native Tax is fixed as from 1 January as follows:

[In the south – 150 *escudos*
In the centre – 85 *escudos*
In the north – 50 *escudos*]

Returning to the narrative of John Bila: 'When I had been working in the house of the Judge, I had earned 50 *escudos* a month, later 75 *escudos*. After ten years in the fortress, I was sent to Lake Niassa to work in the house of the District Officer. I was houseboy, cook and cleaner, and earned 200 *escudos*. In those days a goat cost 80 *escudos*, a tin of rice 30 and an ox 2,000.

In a way, I was lucky to have been sent to the fortress. At least I finished alive. My colleagues who had been sent to other districts such as Malema, Ribaue and Mazerepane, were less fortunate. There in the fortress we had many official visits, and not so many of us were killed. There in the districts, the administrators did whatever they wanted with them and many were beaten to death.

At Lake Niassa, I worked for two years, before my boss returned to Portugal, and I decided to come back to the Island of Mozambique. There was nothing for me in Lourenco Marques. All my force and all my health had been left behind in these streets, in this fortress.

I can never forget that day 29 January 1944 when, already a prisoner, I was herded like a criminal into a packet boat guarded by seven soldiers and a white prison officer, also by a black corporal who was as bad as or even worse than others. These balack corporals and *cipaios* (junior security officials of the administration) had lots of power at that time and were just as bad towards the people as the white colonists were.

Government notice no. 5639 of 29 July 1944: Art. 5. The recruitment of *cipaios* shall take place . . . on a voluntary basis amongst natives who have completed their military service and . . . are less than 30 years of age and more than 1.60m in height.

Government notice no. 4768 of 27 June 1942: Art 2. The following persons shall be exempt from taxes:

4) . . . the wives of local chiefs up to a fixed number;
9) Natives decorated with a cross or medal of military honour;
10) *Cipaio* corporals and auxiliary guards of the civil police.

Government notice no. 4936 of 19 December 1942: Art. 3. The following were exempt from labour service:

1) Local chiefs and headmen of native population groups;
2) Enlisted soldiers while on service;
3) Auxiliaries of chiefs and headmen;
4) *Cipaios*;
5) Corporals.

Government notice no. 4950 of 19 December 1942: Art. 6. The contracting, recruiting, collective transport of any native is not permitted unless such native produces his card.

Para 3. The following need not produce cards if involved in collective transport:
1) While in uniform –

a) Enlisted soldiers and sailors;
b) *Cipaios*;
c) Native auxiliaries and privates in the Fiscal Guard;
d) Corporals and auxiliary guards in the Police Force;
e) Tribal authorities.

The story of John Bila and the recital of the legislation in terms of which he was dealt, illustrate concretely how the 'dualist' legal system fitted into the colonial design. Pluralism in that context meant one set of penal norms for the colonist-master and a completely different set for the colonized-servant. In the sphere of public and civil law, the position was not much different.

The fundamental approach of the colonizer was expressed in the following terms:

> We cannot, for reasons of a practical order, grant to the natives the rights established in our constitutional instruments. We cannot subject the natives' individual, domestic and public life – if we may put it that way – to our political laws, our administrative, civil, commercial and penal codes, to our

> judicial structure. We reserve for them their own legal order in keeping with their faculties, their mentality as primitive people, their feelings, their life, without excluding the need to guide them, in whatever ways possible, to even higher levels of existence . . . It is laid down that private courts be created to give simple, rapid and effective justice to natives. This function is conferred upon the local administrators acting with the collaboration of elements drawn from the local population and with the attendance of the native chiefs, who know the special law of the natives and who are accordingly reliable informants of the uses and traditions of the tribe which need to be referred to in the administration of justice. [Extract from Decree no. 12.533 of 27 November 1926 to establish the political, civil and criminal status of natives in the Portuguese colonies of Angola and Mozambique.]

Art. 4. of the Decree declared that:

> In respect to legal relations between natives, all rights in connection with family law, succession and property shall be regulated in terms of the uses and customs of the population in the region . . . When such regional native uses and customs have not been reduced to writing, they shall be established in each case that goes to trial by means of declarations by the native chief of the area and of two of the most respected natives of the area as designated by the presiding officer of the court.

Art. 9. Natives shall not be granted political rights in relation to institutions that are European in character.

The above law was passed in the period that preceded the coming to power of Dr Salazar. The Salazarist Constitution of 1933, which institutionalized a fascist-type state in Portugal, was accompanied by a Colonial Statute (Law Decree 22465) which outlined the physical boundaries of the Portuguese colonial empire and provided that:

> In the colonies, in keeping with the state of evolution of the native peoples, there will be special statutes for the natives to enable them to establish under the influence of the public and private law of Portugal, legal regimes in harmony with such of their individual, domestic and social uses and customs which are not incompatible with morality and the dictates of humanity.

In 1951, however, with the revision of the 1933 Salazarist Constitution, Portugal made its first major attempt to update itself as a colonial power, and transformed what it had formally called its 'colonies' into what it now called 'Overseas Provinces'.

The new emphasis was on a Portugal united and indivisible, with equality for all its citizens; alleging a common pride in being Portuguese and blurring somewhat the earlier distinctions between 'civilized citizens', on the one hand, and 'primitive natives' on the other.

Thus Art. 133 of the law to revise the 1933 Constitution (Law no. 2048 of 23 June 1951) declared that:

> It is of the organic essence of the Portuguese Nation to carry out the historic function of colonizer of the lands of the Discoveries under its sovereignty and to transmit to and diffuse amongst the populations that exist in these lands the benefits of its civilization, exercising as well the moral influence which emanates from the trusteeship (tutelage) of the west.

Article 134 added that:

> The overseas territories of Portugal . . . are generically referred to as 'Provinces' and have a political–administrative organization suited to their geographical situation and the conditions of the social environment.

Notes

1. A fuller selection can be found in the first edition of the Ministry of Justice's journal – *Justica Popular* (1979).
2. This village, in the coastal zone of the north of Mozambique, about 1,600 kilometres from Maputo, is famous for its basket-makers' co-operative. It is in an area in which Islamic influence is strong.
3. These titles have been added.
4. In the original, the names of the parties were given.
5. Three hundred *escudos* were worth about 10 US dollars at the time. The currency has since been changed to *meticais*.
6. A member of the colonial police.
7. There is no adequate translation for the word *responsavel*. It means the person who has responsibility for a certain function or in relation to a certain area, and in the context could refer to members of the village administration or members of the Women's Movement or Youth Movement.
8. The village does not have a prison, so even in cases of assault, theft and so on, the court will order community service, such as weeding the public square, or building a schoolroom, for a specified period of days.
9. At that time the word 'comrade' was widely used in the courts as elsewhere as a normal form of designation. After criticism by President Samora Machel that the term was being abused ('will the comrade murderer please come forward'), its use was confined to strictly political contexts only.
10. Because there is no one who can help us resolve this dilemma.
11. This is an example of how norms are established through oral 'orientations'.

5. The Bride Price, Revolution, and the Liberation of Women*

Introduction

Vulande, who was an only daughter, had her bride price paid by an Indian. At that time Indian merchants did not bring their families with them when they came to trade in Africa. Vulande had a daughter but her husband died and she returned to her parents' home. Some time later, Vulande had her second bride price paid by a man called Massinga with whom she later had two sons. However, the sons died and she, falling out with her husband, returned once more to her parents' home. In the meantime, Vulande's father, Mutxeketxa Hunguana, who was a warrior in the anti-colonial resistance, was in Gaza where he participated in the battle of Magul, on the side of Gungunhana's troops fighting against Portuguese domination. After the war Mutxeketxa returned to his birthplace, Marracuene. Finding everything laid waste by the Portuguese colonialists, the lands devastated, cattle dead, he decided to found a new settlement and begin life again near the beautiful lagoon of Molongotiva.

Vulande, wishing to ease the sadness of her father, paid on his behalf the bride price of a widow called Mi Hambene, who had already had a daughter from a previous marriage. However, Vulande's father died without having any more children. According to the rules of the bride price (*lobolo*) Mi Hambene was 'inherited' by Nwa Massangalane, paternal cousin of Vulande, with whom she had a daughter, Babalala. Later, because she was ill-treated by Nwa Massangalane, Mi Hambene left his house. Thus, Vulande assumed the right of control over Babalala because she was born during the period when the bride price that had been paid for her was still in force.

Later on, Mi Hambene went to live with another man called Nwa Vilanculo, but refused to let him pay her bride price, seeing that the obligations relating to the bride price with the Hunguanas had not yet been complied with. Mi Hambene had children with Nwa Vilanculo. When the first daughter Hlonipane had her price of £35 sterling paid, it was Vilanculo who by right received the bride price.

When Vulande died, this money was inherited by her only male child Raul

* A shortened version of this article was published in the *International Journal of the Sociology of Law*, 15, 1987, pp. 369–92.

Honwana, whom she had had in a later marriage with Manuel Honwana (Nwa Npunana) in 1905. However, when Raul Honwana married for the first time in 1927, the father of his fiancée, who was a Church dignitary, refused to accept the bride price and the £35 sterling was used instead by Raul Honwane, the bridegroom, to build the house where he went to live with his wife.

In May 1940, Raul Honwana married for the second time (first in Church and then at the registry office) and eight and a half years later, his wife Naly Nhaca had her fifth child, and so was born the author of this work.[1]

This rich and complex family history, of the kind that could be repeated in tens of thousands of Mozambican homes, forms the personal background against which this study has been conducted. Although Gita Welch's parents themselves belong to families that rejected *lobolo* as a system, and although both are firmly committed to the goals of the revolution, there can be no doubt that at the cultural and emotional levels they still retain affection for the ways of doing things of their parents' parents and that the concept of *lobolo* is by no means dead in their hearts.

The professional background against which this study is being undertaken is that, as a judge of the Provincial People's Tribunal, and later as head of the Department of Research and Legislation, one of the authors has for a number of years been called upon to follow the principle that

> marriage is not a business transaction, and does not have as its object the exchange of any material advantage to the bride or groom or families . . . In particular, the state fights against the giving of any consideration in the form of *lobolo* . . .[2]

The *lobolo* contemplated by this declaration was in essence a set of socially sanctioned and specifically agreed dealings between two families whereby the prospective groom transfers material goods or carries out specified services in favour of the family of the bride, and as a result of which the bride passes into the family of the groom, subordinating or integrating her will and interests to those of her husband, and accepting the establishment of a relationship of possession or ownership between the children and the father. Such transactions have had three fundamental characteristics. In the first place they have constituted a sophisticated and time-honoured process deeply rooted in the culture of large sections of the Mozambican people by means of which social recognition is accorded to marriage (the cultural dimension).

Secondly, they have involved the transfer of material values, either in the form of goods or of services, on the part of the groom in favour of the family of the bride (the economic dimension).

Thirdly, they have formed the basis for a series of legal relationships not only between the groom and bride but between their respective families, governing such questions as property regimes, divorce, rights over children, and rights of succession (the legal dimension).

As we shall see, *lobolo* takes on different forms in different parts of the country, and always has a variety of meanings that go well beyond the mere 'commercialization of' (trade in) brides. The problem of this study, therefore, is to determine the politico-legal strategy that needs to be pursued at this stage in order to enable the different elements of the phenomenon known as *lobolo* to be disentangled, ensuring that the aspects that are negative and harmful can be combated, while those that are positive can be incorporated into the revolutionary process.

In this respect, it is noteworthy that a number of strategies have already been advanced over the years in relation to *lobolo*, which may be summarized as follows:

(a) the conservative strategy which argues that, as an intrinsic part of the people's culture, *lobolo* should be preserved. Here we may find three sub-groups with different reasons for wishing to preserve the institution, namely, those who feel deeply and genuinely that *lobolo* is an integral part of their world-view, of their way of doing things, of their culture; those who, anxious to obtain the maximum material benefit from marrying off their daughters, speak forcefully and more opportunistically about defending the people's culture; and those Africanist scholars who argue that traditional law represents the authentic juridical world-view of the people, and that the true grassroots laws must be defended against the onslaughts both of colonial law imposed directly by the colonialists and of neo-colonial law imposed by an alienated indigenous post-colonial elite. Whatever their different motives, the conservatives all wish to see *lobolo* recognized and applied as an ongoing sytem of norms by the courts;

(b) the abolitionist strategy, which defines *lobolo* as a social evil, a relic of past feudal social relationships, which has to be eliminated root and branch in all its different forms and ramifications, using the criminal law if necessary to achieve this end;

(c) the regulative strategy, which presupposes that there is nothing wrong with the practice of *lobolo* itself, save that abuses have set in with regard to the amounts claimed, which therefore need to be controlled by means of imposing legal ceilings;

(d) the neutralist or protective strategy, in terms of which *lobolo* is something which belongs to the people outside of the sphere of state intervention; as such it may be studied ethnographically, but the only appropriate strategy available to the state is that of having no strategy at all.

For reasons which will be more fully developed at a later stage, the writers reject all these particular strategies as being in each case scientifically invalid and socially harmful, and will argue instead for a politico-legal strategy which, while embracing elements of conservation, abolition, regulation and neutralism, is quite at variance in philosophy and implementation from any of these. However, in order to situate the argument in the concrete socio-cultural reality of Mozambique, it is necessary first to examine the many and varied dimensions of the phenomenon so widely denounced and so widely defended under the general denomination *lobolo*.

The Various Dimensions of *Lobolo*

In his classic study of the Tsonga[3] people who inhabit the southern portion of Mozambique the Swiss missionary Henri Jounod devoted considerable attention to the topic of *lobolo*.

In the first part of his book, in his capacity as scientist wishing to make an accurate record, he sets out the history and principal characteristics of the phenomenon, while in the conclusion, in his capacity as missionary, 'seeking to improve the life of the people' amongst whom he worked, he makes a number of proposals for 'dealing' with it. According to oral tradition, he points out, there never was a period in which *lobolo* did not exist. What changed over the years was the form that *lobolo* took, from reed carpets in times pre-dating the arrival of the first European traders, to large copper or iron rings acquired from European sailors, to so many handfuls of beads, followed by cattle in the eighteenth century, until the stocks were so diminished by war that they were replaced by hoes and then, in the late nineteenth century, by 'the more powerful Pound Sterling', this latter being converted into guineas when it had been learnt that civilized people used guineas. *Lobolo*, therefore, came to have two separate sources in respect of a young man intending to marry: that derived from the marriage of his sister, which he in his turn could use to get a bride, and that which he earned from his own work, for example, on the mines in Johannesburg.

The only way to understand *lobolo*, Jounod argues, is that it represents a form of contract between two families in which compensation is offered by the groom's family to the bride's family in respect of their loss of a member (pp. 121 and 268), enabling the latter thereby to acquire another woman in her place. The bride thereby passes to a new family, to whom she and all her children will belong. Though by no means a slave, she is nevertheless a kind of property, not of her husband as such, but of his family as a whole. Thus, the whole of the bride's family takes part in the wedding ceremonies, with a right to pass comment on the cattle or goods offered, while on the groom's side, all his brothers will help in the collection of the necessary cattle or goods; the bride therefore belongs to her brothers-in-law as well, though she will not have sexual relations with any of them unless she passes by inheritance on the death of her husband. In the meanwhile, the children of the marriage belong to and owe the father obedience, the sons living with him and strengthening his group, and the daughters being sold into marriage for his financial benefit.

Jounod remarks that in what he calls the primary collective stage of society, *lobolo* has certain great advantages: it strengthens the family, especially the patriarchal family; it distinguishes a lawful marriage from an unlawful one, and in this respect acts as substitute for an official Register; and it discourages the easy dissolution of a marriage, inasmuch as a woman may not leave her husband without her family restoring *lobolo*.

These advantages, however, should not be exaggerated, he adds, because *lobolo* does not protect a woman from ill-treatment by her husband, nor does it prevent many marriages from breaking up (witness the history of this author's foreparents as cited earlier).

There are two disagreeable consequences of *lobolo*. One, the woman concerned is definitely diminished as a person because she is being paid for. This starts before her marriage, where it is her family who chooses her groom on this basis of his capacity to pay *lobolo*, or perhaps to settle an ancient family debt. Fortunately, Jounod declares, man is often better than his principles, and frequently the bride's wishes will be taken into account. The woman then works for her husband, for little recompense; she is forbidden to sleep with any other man, but he is free to sleep with whom he pleases because he has not been paid for; the children of the marriage belong to him even if she is an excellent mother and he a poor father; and on her husband's death, she may be passed on like a species of property to one of his brothers. Second, disputes over the size and payment of *lobolo* can keep families at arm's length for generations, especially when it is a case of seeking restitution of *lobolo* after a woman has left her husband. A question of a few pounds can poison life among the people in a whole zone; it is *lobolo* that accounts for three-quarters of all cases brought before court, Jounod observes.

If in his capacity as ethnographer, but more as a person of sensitivity who lived among and worked with the people of southern Mozambique, Jounod reveals a certain measure of respect mixed in with his criticisms of *lobolo*, in his capacity as missionary his position is quite firm: the struggle against *lobolo* is an absolute, and he cannot understand these missionaries who feel that the Church should adopt a tolerant attitude towards it. He stresses that the material nature of *lobolo* deprives a truly Christian marriage of its foundation in mutual love, and, secondly, that *lobolo* is intimately bound up with polygamy, since it leads to widows being inherited by brothers-in-law already married, and to men who have many sisters and few brothers taking for themselves as many wives as they have surplus sisters. For these reasons, he declares that no Christian father may demand *lobolo* for his daughter, Christian widows are free, and may keep their children without going to their brothers-in-law, and mothers have the same rights to their children as have fathers. However, if a Christian man marries a pagan woman, he must pay *lobolo* to the bride's father, but not so as to expect any of the rights which flow from this.

If all missionaries were agreed on these principles, he states confidently, the practice of *lobolo* would rapidly disappear. But, in the meanwhile, the State has a role to play – provided it does not try to impose its own values on a conquered people – in hastening the disappearance of this deplorable custom. It should create a marriage register to establish the legitimacy of marriages, whether or not *lobolo* has been paid; it should fix a low maximum payment (though the danger exists of excess payments being made clandestinely); a law could be passed enabling widows to remain free and in charge of their children; and the authorities could proclaim the principle that when the father or the older brother of the bride renounces *lobolo*, no other member of the family should have the right to claim it in their stead.

Finally, Jounod mentions the half-way house measure adopted by many

Christians of giving a present instead of *lobolo*, 'to assuage the heart of the father losing his daughter'. But the father's heart is never assuaged, he declares, and the matter lingers on to create tension.

Viewed in the context of time, for all its paternalism and assumptions about the superiority of Western civilization, Jounod's work must be seen as an outstanding piece of observation written by a person imbued with respect for the society he was studying. It certainly stood in sharp contrast to the normal colonial vilifications of traditional society, in which the indigenous people were referred to as living in a state of brute savagery outside any conceptions of law and morality.

However, despite the efforts of churchpeople like Jounod, *lobolo* continued to enjoy great support among the people, and the dramatic choice posed by Jounod between what he regarded as the Christian individualist world-view and the pagan collectivist world-view continued with unabating intensity from generation to generation. Many otherwise loyal churchmen failed the test. They organized Church and civil marriages for their daughters, and then 'assuaged their hearts' by accepting cattle and money as well. It was not simply a question of covetousness, it was a question of obtaining social acceptance for the marriage.

> To take a woman home without *lobolo* was equivalent to abduction. Even if he did so many years later, the man had to pay *lobolo* to the woman's family if he wished the marriage to be socially accepted. [Interview with Raul Honwana]

These are the words of a bride of that time, whose father, a Christian, had been put to the test, and in fact had won through.

> Even her family had no respect for their son-in-law. And the woman herself felt quite unprotected, she had no guarantees at all, the man could send her away at any moment. On the other hand, if she had been purchased (*lobolo*-ed), the question had to be fully debated before there could be a divorce, in particular, the goods paid by the man in respect of the bride price had to be restored. [Ibid.]

Dealing with her own situation, our informant explains that it was the parents who had decided whether *lobolo* should be paid or not. At that time, gold was already scarce, and *lobolo* was paid in Portuguese currency in the amount of 2,500 *escudos*, but this was preceded by a formal marriage request (*kubuta*) which cost 500 *escudos*, a silk scarf and a ring.

> Most of my friends had their bride price paid, but in my case my father, who was an elder of the Wesleyan Church and was also assimilated, did not want *lobolo*, so I was married only in the registry office and the church. Many other churchmen, however, accepted *lobolo* for their daughters as well as having a religious wedding, while those living in the city went through the registry office ceremony in addition. [Ibid.]

Her husband adds that his previous marriage had also been without *lobolo*, since his first wife's father had been a preacher in the Presbyterian Church (Swiss Mission) and that when as a widower he remarried, he used the £35 sterling he had inherited from his mother to build a family house rather than pay *lobolo*, since his father-in-law was also against *lobolo*.

An interesting aspect of our informants' recollections was that, although imbued with the anti-*lobolo* tradition, they both retained a deep respect for the institution, insisting merely that what had once been good had been debased by Portuguese colonialism. The quantity of articles paid in respect of the *lobolo*, whether hoes, seeds, copper bracelets, cattle or sterling was an indicator of the social level of both the man who paid and the woman who was paid for. What the colonialists did was to monetarize the transaction completely, and manipulate it in order to control the movement of cattle. Thus in 1930 the Director of Native Affairs decreed that the limit for *lobolo* be 2,500 *escudos* in cash, or 4,000 *escudos* in the case of a chief's daughter. Although the reason given was that there were too many quarrels amongst 'the natives' over *lobolo*, the real objective of the decree was to stop the movement of cattle from family to family and so enable the authorities to maintain control of the livestock.

> The colonialists were not interested in the substantive questions relating to traditional marriage, such as the age of consent, polygamy, divorce. They weren't worried about child marriages or multiple marriages or abandoned wives, all they were concerned about was the geographical location of herds of cattle in a given region. Thus before registering their marriages, the people would have to register their cattle, and only then would the *lobolo* be registered under the heading 'native marriage' or 'kaffir marriage'. [Ibid.]

Lobolo Today in Mozambique

Lobolo continues as an institution in a variety of forms in contemporary Mozambique. In popular language, *lobolo* is the term used to connote any material advantage given in respect of the acquisition of a bride, whether it takes the form of cattle, money, goods, or services, and whether it passes to the bride's parents or the bride herself. Basically we may discern three forms of marriage settlement all loosely, if unscientifically, referred to as *lobolo*.

1. The payment of cattle, money or goods in the southern and central areas of the country, traditionally cattle keeping patrilineal societies. In Manica Province there is a variant in that a down-payment is made to the bride's parents and the full sum only becomes due when the bride's child-bearing capacity has been proved. The process of determining the exact extent of the *lobolo* can be drawn out as in any peasant marriage settlement negotiation in the world, and it would not be unusual to find a long list of items negotiated in cash and kind, ending with such objects as one gross of tins of condensed milk. The total value may well exceed 50,000 *meticais*.

2. The rendering of services by the groom in favour of the bride's family. This is the most common form in the central areas of the country, traditionally

matrilineal and matrilocal agricultural societies, in which the husband works for an agreed period, usually two or three years, on the fields of his in-laws in consideration for marrying their daughter and settling in their area. This practice is found in Zambezia, in Nampula, and in Tete where both matrilineal and patrilineal societies are to be found, so that in one part of the province a groom will move to his wife's homestead and perform services there, knowing that his children will belong to his wife's family rather than his, while in another he will pay between 6,000 and 7,000 *meticais* as *ntsambo* to receive the bride into his home, with the knowledge that the children will belong to his family and not hers. In many traditionally matrilineal areas a tendency can be noted for the son-in-law to pay cash rather than perform the services, and this may be associated with a certain loosening of the strict rules of matrilinearity.

3. The payment of a dowry in cash or precious ornaments to the bride or her parents. This is most common in the central and northern areas where Islamic influence is strong, such as in the coastal parts of Sofala, Zambezia, Nampula and Cabo Delgado, and in Niassa Province. Called *mahari*, it varies from 500 to 5,000 *meticais* and is normally paid on the day of the marriage ceremony (*nikah*).

Each of these three basic modes of constituting a marriage carried with it its own set of traditional legal consequences, and whatever the formal legal status of such rules might be today, there can be no doubt that they are still of considerable influence in guiding the way people resolve family disputes, name their children, and pass on family property. We may thus speak of three basic sets or complexes of rules, the first of which relates to *lobolo* properly so-called, the second to the performance of services in the matrilineal societies, the third to the application of the rules of the Koran, as adapted to the local conditions. The focus of this study is on the first in which the controversial element of 'bride price' is most pronounced. While the overall strategy in relation to the other two would be the same, there are great practical and legal differences which would require substantially different methodologies as far as practical implementation is concerned. These would belong to a separate study – this study concentrates on the question of the strategy to be adopted in relation to the bride wealth paid in the traditionally patrilineal societies in the southern part of the country, a subject that has aroused strong feeling over the years, and the resolution of which remains as yet without final determination.

Lobolo and the Liberation of Women

> The emancipation of women is not an act of charity, the result of a humanitarian or compassionate attitude. The liberation of women is a fundamental necessity for the revolution, the guarantee of its continuity, and the precondition for its eventual triumph.

With these now famous words pronounced at the opening of the First Conference of Mozambican Women in 1973, Samora Machel, President of

Frelimo, placed the question of the liberation of women in the forefront of the armed struggle for national independence. In rebuttal of the arguments that a failure to respect certain local traditions would result in a loss of support from the masses, and that in any event to emancipate women when women themselves were indifferent to the matter would be an artificial imposition, Samora Machel declared that the armed struggle itself had created the conditions for the masses to be receptive to the ideas of progress and revolution.

It was true, he said, that women's exploitation could only be understood within the context of the general system of exploitation of man by man. But women were exploited workers with special characteristics. To possess women was to possess unpaid labourers whose entire output would be appropriated without resistance by the husband, who was lord and master. In an agrarian economy marrying many women was a guarantee of accumulating a great deal of wealth. The husband was assured of free labour which neither complained nor rebelled against exploitation.

Hence the important role of polygamy in the rural areas of an underdeveloped agrarian economy.

> Society, realizing that women are a source of wealth, demands that a price be paid for them. The girl's parents demand from their future son-in-law the payment of a bride price – *lobolo* – before giving up their daughter. The woman is bought and inherited just like material goods, or any source of wealth. (OMM, 1983).

Unlike other unpaid workers, however, the woman offered her owner two added advantages: she was a source of pleasure, and she produced other workers. This last aspect was particularly important since society granted the husband the right to repudiate his wife and demand the repayment of *lobolo* should she prove barren. This excessive emphasis on fertility led to the transformation of the man–woman relationship into that of the mere act of procreation. The question of inheritance became central. An exploiter might, owing to his control of the masses, acquire vast estates and large herds of cattle, but still he would be mortal, and the problem arose of the fate of his wealth. Women were the producers of his heirs.

The transformation of women into producers without rights, in the service of their husbands or fathers, involved a corresponding ideology and culture, together with an educational system for their transmission. Rites and ceremonies were the main vehicle for the transmission of society's concept of women's inferiority and their subservience to men. The process of alienation reached its peak when the exploited person was no longer capable of even imagining that the possibility of liberation existed.

Samora Machel insisted that the fundamental and antagonistic contradiction was not between women and men, but between women and the social order, but he went on to add that secondary contradictions such as those that arose between men and women because of the marriage system, marital authority based solely on gender, the frequent brutality of husbands and their refusal to treat their wives as equals, could produce serious consequences if not correctly dealt with.

Turning to the 'new revolutionary concept of the couple and the home', he concluded that the family relationship, the man–woman relationship, should be founded exclusively on love.

> We do not mean the banal, romantic concept of love which amounted to little more than emotional excitement and an idealized view of life. For us love can only exist between free and equal people who have the same ideas and commitment in serving the masses and the revolution. This is the basis upon which the moral and emotional affinity which constitutes love is built. We need to discover this new dimension, hitherto unknown in our country.[4]

The question of *lobolo* thus became a national issue not in the context of the great moral choice projected by Jounod as between paganism and Christianity, as between the collective and the individual world-view, as between the allegedly lower and an allegedly higher form of civilization, but in terms of the great popular debate initiated by the revolutionary leadership at a time when the Mozambican people were struggling, arms in hand, to destroy foreign domination, forge themselves into a nation, and achieve independent statehood. *Lobolo* was linked with polygamy and child marriages as features of what was called traditional/feudal society, one that stifled the creative capacity of the people by subordinating commoners to chiefs, the young to the old – and women and men. The fact that large portions of Mozambican territory were being converted into liberated zones in which new social structures and patterns of consciousness were being developed meant that the new perspectives had immediate practical impact, being applied as basic guidelines for the embryonic state structures that were evolving. The question of *lobolo* was therefore posed as a question for the revolution. Men and women came from all parts of the country to take part in the liberation war. When they married it was with the consciousness not of belonging to this or that ethnic group or of coming from this or that region, but of being creators of the new Mozambique. What had formerly been patriotic, namely defence of the local tradition against the assimilationist pressures of colonialism, now became an obstacle to the development of a wider and more dynamic patriotism that would be based on the conception of the nation as a whole. The creation of a national consciousness therefore encompassed a profound process of cultural transformation which entered into the details of daily life, overturning long-held beliefs on such intimate questions as diet and hygiene, while at the same time offering the wider perspective of a revolutionary national identity.

The building up of the Women's Detachment in the Liberation Army had a particularly profound impact, since a woman dressed in military uniform bearing an AK rifle and entering villages to organize food production and the transport of weapons was hardly suitable as the subject of *lobolo*. Men from the south who had come to fight in the north had no means of paying *lobolo* to women from the north even if they wished to do so – the pledge they offered was their determination to fight for independence rather than cattle, goods, or services. At the same time, major institutional changes were taking place in what came to be known as the liberated zones, those increasingly large areas that by the war's end encompassed nearly two million people. The incapacity of traditional power to identify with and incorporate itself into the liberation struggle — indeed, the tendency of the chiefs and *indunas* to ally themselves with the colonial authorities, whether through tax collecting, recruitment for forced labour, or supplying intelligence on Frelimo activities — resulted in the complete elimination of the institutions of traditional power in the liberated zones and their replacement by organs of popular power. The mass meeting, organized by the Liberation Army, and subject to the principles of free speech and active popular involvement, became the main means of resolving disputes.

The following is just one example of how a family law question was handled.

> A husband and wife had separated, and the husband's family and the wife both wanted custody of the children. The husband's family argued that since *lobolo* (or its equivalent) had been paid, the children belonged as of right to them. The wife said that her husband was a drunkard and an informer for the colonialists, and that it was better that the children grew up with her. The meeting debated the issue for some hours before deciding by consensus that if the traditional law clashed with the new principles of the revolutionary struggle for independence, then it was the new principles that had to prevail.

In some areas the question of *lobolo* itself was sharply debated. Soldiers, often from other parts of the country, fell in love with local young women. In Niassa province, the *lobolo* was merely symbolic, the transfer of beads, but in parts of Tete the parents demanded money or cattle, as many as fifteen head.

> In a war situation [recalls one guerrilla commander] we had neither goods nor money to offer. Some parents accepted a symbolic present, such as a length of cloth, but demanded that after independence was gained 'real' *lobolo* should be paid. There was one case in which one of our soldiers was neither able nor willing to pay the ten head of cattle demanded, so the bride's parents requested as an alternative that he clear a field and prepare two oxen for the ploughing. This is an arduous and time-consuming task . . . so we had to intervene explaining that he had urgent military tasks to attend to . . . and finally the parents accepted the marriage without any payment (interview with José Moiane, Governor of the Province of Maputo, December 1983, in *Justiça Popular*, no. 8–9, January–June 1984).

The result of the accumulation of such experiences over many years and in a large part of the country was that by the time independence was achieved, a clear set of principles, procedures, and institutions for dealing with family matters had already been established. It is important to stress, therefore, that the 'model' which was to serve for independent Mozambique was not derived from the former Metropole (Portugal), nor from an idealized version of marriage as contained in Church doctrine, nor from an idealized version of revolutionary practice as experienced in other countries. It grew from the practice of the liberated zones in Mozambique itself, in which the organized peasantry established the embryo of the new state and in which a generation of new leaders with new ideas and experience of government emerged even before independence was won.

The Legal Status of *Lobolo* Today

Inspired by experience in the liberated zones, the Constitution of the People's Republic of Mozambique contains no less than four articles dealing with the necessity to combat inequality between men and women. In the section entitled General Principles, one of the fundamental objectives of the country is declared to be the elimination of the structures of colonial and traditional oppression and exploitation and the mentalities that go with them (Art. 4). Also in this section is a provision that is constitutionally unique in that it speaks explicitly of the liberation of women:

> The liberation of women is one of the essential tasks of the State. In the People's Republic of Mozambique a woman is equal to a man in terms of rights and duties, such equality extending to the political, economic, social, and cultural spheres.

In the section dealing with the fundamental rights and duties of citizens, the theme of equal rights is repeated twice:

> All Mozambican citizens enjoy the same rights and are subject to the same duties irrespective of colour, race, sex, ethnic origin, place of birth, religion, degree of education, social position, or profession. (Art. 26).

This Article is particularly important because it contains no saving clause such as that found in other African constitutions where distinctions are permitted in relation to family matters and land use based on customary law or religion. In other words, Mozambique has opted for a unitary rather than a pluralistic approach to legal rights and duties, making ethnicity or religion completely irrelevant in relation to the exercise of judicial power (see Art. 72). Ethnic diversity and multilinguism are highly important as the material substance from which the new Mozambican cultural personality is fashioned (Art. 15), but they are not to be taken directly into account when it comes to the exercise of popular political and judicial power.

Lastly, Art. 29 reaffirms that women and men are to enjoy the same rights and be subject to the same duties. 'This principle is to guide all legislative and executive action by the State. The State protects marriage, the family, maternity, and infancy.'

Taken in conjunction, the above provisions indicate, first, that the question of equality between women and men is regarded as being one of the fundamental questions of the Constitution, and second, that the achievement of equality is seen as being dependent not simply on the affirmation of equal rights but on the elimination of the structures of women's oppression. Third, the emphasis on unity and on the need to 'eliminate divisiveness based on ethnic distinctions' suggests that a unitary rather than a pluralistic strategy is contemplated in the important area of family rights. Finally, the absence of any express mention of specific institutions such as child marriages, polygamy, initiation rites, and *lobolo*, indicates that a certain degree of flexibility is contemplated with regard to the specific modes whereby 'structures of oppression' are to be combated and equality achieved.

In fact, looking at the first ten years after independence, two distinctive phases can be seen. In the first five years a strong campaign on the cultural and political levels was conducted against what were called the evils of polygamy, child marriages, and *lobolo*. Thus the anthem of the Women's Movement, repeatedly heard on the radio and sung at branch meetings in every town and village in the country, denounced *lobolo*.

The slogans *Abaixo poligamia! Abaixo casamentos prematuros! Abaixo lobolo!* were heard at countless gatherings, mingled with denunciations of racism, colonialism, and imperialism. *Lobolo* was not only considered an evil in itself: it was seen as the mechanics for the perpetuation of further evils, such as child marriages (early *lobolo*) and polygamy (multiple *lobolo*). At the same time, however, the authorities were at pains to ensure that the power of the state was never used to suppress what was seen to be essentially a cultural phenomenon with deep historical roots.

It is precisely in a situation of major social and cultural transformation that the usefulness and limitations of the law as an instrument of social control and social change become most evident. In the case of *lobolo* the strategy of the law was neither to recognize nor to penalize, but rather deliberately to ignore the institution. The State denounced but did not suppress it. *Lobolo* was not illegal, in the sense that no one could be punished for paying or receiving it. But nor at the same time was it 'legal'. The courts said in effect that *lobolo* was a social transaction that might have meaning for the parties involved and even for the community to which they belong, but that it had no legal significance as far as state institutions were concerned; thus people engaging in the transaction did so knowing full well that they could never use it as the basis for founding a legal claim. Neither the groom nor his in-laws could sue for cattle to be paid or to be restored; neither groom nor bride could sue for divorce and concomitant restitution or retention of cattle on the basis of the rules associated with *lobolo*; neither husband nor wife could base a claim for custody of the children on whether *lobolo* had been paid or not; none could base an inheritance claim on the payment or otherwise of *lobolo* by parents or grandparents. Thus the courts not only refused to recognize and give effect to the *lobolo* undertaking itself, they also refused to apply the whole subsidiary network of *lobolo*-related legal norms in situations in which family law problems arose because of family breakdown, whether such breakdown resulted from separation or death.

In fact, a large portion of the community continued to constitute and dissolve their families in terms of the rules of *lobolo*, doing so outside the state system. But there were also many cases where the informal or non-state sector of justice failed to resolve disputes, and where recourse was had to the courts or to other state or political structures. The question of the normative base used by the state courts for the resolution of such cases will be dealt with at a later stage, when consideration is given to the Family Law Project. Suffice to say at this stage that the existence of *lobolo* might have been indirectly relevant as to whether or not a *de facto* union existed, but it certainly did not determine the rules for how the dispute was to be settled.

At one stage in the period immediately after independence, when few new court structures existed, such family disputes would be classified as social problems to be resolved by the appropriate committee of the local dynamizing group (as the nucleus of Frelimo supporters in each locality was called). With the establishment from 1978 onwards of an extensive network of people's tribunals, however, problems of family breakdown came increasingly to be heard by judges in formally constituted courts. In fact, about two-thirds of all cases coming before the people's tribunals at the level of the rural locality or urban neighbourhood have tended to be based on family disputes. The judges were elected from the local community and almost invariably in a bench of from three to five, at least one leading member of the Women's Movement would be included. Frequently illiterate, the judges relied neither on the Portuguese Codes nor on traditional (customary) law, but instead tried to reconcile the parties, and, if this failed, determined cases 'in accordance with good sense and taking into account the principles guiding the building of a socialist society' (12 October 1978, section 38). In practice, when the courts were established (usually at a public meeting in a festive atmosphere) the judges and all those present were given general guidance by representatives of the Ministry of Justice as to what principles they should apply, namely to facilitate the departure of unhappy wives from polygamies, and to try to keep monogamous marriages alive, save that if such marriages were in a state of serious breakdown, the judges could decree a divorce and ensure an equitable division of the family property, and see to best possible provisions for the children.

A preliminary survey of the practice of these courts in the first seven years of their existence suggests that, in general, they apply these principles without strain, making no reference to the way the marriage was constituted, whether by traditional procedures or religious ceremony or simply by the parties living together, but simply accepting the marriage as a marriage. The payment or otherwise of *lobolo* is not referred to, neither in determining whether a marriage exists (normally a notorious fact in the community, the judges knowing full well who are regarded as husband and wife), nor in relation to a claim for payment of restitution of cattle or other goods (such a claim would not be admitted), nor in relation to the rules governing divorce or succession (where the principles of good sense outlined previously would be applied). It may be that indirectly and in areas where the *lobolo* tradition is particularly strong, the judge's sentiments as to what constitutes good sense in relation to custody of children or to division of property might, in a particular case, be influenced by the background of *lobolo*; that is, the existence of *lobolo* might be regarded as having some evidential value relative to the solution of problems, but the problems are, however, posed in non-*lobolo* terms. Overwhelmingly it seems that the new judges apply new principles in terms of codes of behaviour that are consistent with the principles of the Constitution, in keeping with the 'launching' orientations of the Ministry of Justice and the more or less regular guidelines of the higher courts, and in line with general popular sentiment as to what is equitable between person and person in a concrete case. Similarly, the approach is roughly the same, whether in the north, centre, or south of the country, whether in the countryside or in the town. A few illustrative examples of actual decisions can be given here, derived from both authors' experiences of working and observing in the new court. (Our impression is that the division of property is frequently what brings the parties to the court – people come together and separate without the aid of formal state institutions, but when they and their families fail to agree on the division of their property, or when the father fails to make provision for his children, recourse may be had to the tribunals.)

Cases Heard in Community Courts at the Local Level

1. *The House*. Maputo city in a poor area, houses of reed and zinc. The wife complained that her husband was abandoning her and that he wanted to take all the zinc sheets of their house with him. The tribunal ordered that she should keep two-thirds of the zinc sheets, and that he was to pay one-third of his salary for the children. If he did not pay regularly to the court, an order would be made that his employers deduct the amount from his salary.

2. *The Plough*. In a rural area on the outskirts of Xai-Xai, capital of Gaza Province. A man lived in a polygamous union with two women, M1 and M2, for ten years in the same area. He was a peasant and he and his wives worked a plot of two hectares, using a plough and team of oxen. In addition, each wife had her own vegetable plot.

The problem was how to distribute the property on the man's death. Each of his widows wished to remarry and they agreed that they should live in separate homes. The case was referred to the 'structures' of the communal neighbourhood, who in turn referred the matter to the tribunal.

The decision of the tribunal was that M1 should keep the house and the family field, and that the inhabitants of the area should build two new huts for M2, one for sleeping in and one for cooking in, and also open up a new field of one hectare for her. The plough and oxen would continue to be at the disposal of both widows.

3. *The Clothes*. In a rural area in Sofala Province. W. alleged that one day her drunken husband H. threatened to beat her up, and when she fled he burnt her clothes, namely, one dress, two pieces of material, three *capulanas* (decorated cloth used as skirt), and two blouses.

The tribunal decided that H. had to buy all these clothes for W. and that he would have to perform seven days of community service and 'do some work for the people'. After this decision was pronounced, the couple said they did not want each other any more. H. refused to accept the judgement, and so the case was referred on appeal to the district tribunal.

4. *The Child's Needs.* Rural district in Zambezia Province. The Complainant said she had had a child with the Defendant, who had refused to marry her. D. had not attended to the needs of the child. Having heard the evidence of those who knew the couple, the tribunal decided that D. was the father, and that he should sign a document acknowledging the fact, and buy food and clothes for the child as well as for C.; also, that he should be with his child from time to time.

5. *The House.* In Pemba, capital of Cabo Delgado Province, in an area of well-constructed pole and mud houses. H. and W. had one child and wished to divorce each other. Their respective families had been unable to reach an agreement and so had referred the case to the Muslim judicial structure, which had also failed to produce an agreed solution. Accordingly, the matter was sent to the tribunal which decided that W. and the child should stay on in the family home, but that W.'s family should pay to H. half the value of the house so that he could build a new one for himself.

The Family Law Project

Although the Project was drafted basically by lawyers and judges in the higher reaches of the Ministry of Justice, its key provisions – or 'options' as they were called – reflected the already existing practice of the community courts at the local level. This can be seen in relation to four fundamental questions: the concept of marriage; attitude to *lobolo*; divorce; and *de facto* unions.

The traditional courts had treated marriage essentially as an alliance between two families; the colonial courts had adopted the hybrid conception contained in the Portuguese Civil Code in terms of which marriage was regarded as a sacrament, an institution with assigned sexual roles, and a proprietary contract. The people's tribunals adopted the quite different concept of a voluntary union based on equality and the free assumption by the partners of rights and responsibilities. Although the judges might not always have expressed themselves exactly in these terms, these were the principles that underlay their decisions, as a study of court records shows, and these are the principles that are firmly declared in the opening articles of the Project.

Lobolo was, of course, central to the operation of the traditional courts in family matters. The colonial courts had largely ignored it, relegating it to the sphere of 'uses and customs' to be determined by the district administrator in consultation with those whom he [always a man in colonial times] regarded as trustworthy elders. The local people's tribunals simply ignored the *lobolo* aspect of the question, but looked to the reality of the union and attempted to give practical solutions to practical questions. The Family Law

Project, which in addition to its normative and instrumental provisions, had a number of articles of a clearly programmatic kind, went a step further and declared:

> Marriage, which is an act based exclusively on the free wish of both parties, does not permit of any interference to force its realization. Marriage is not a business transaction nor is it destined to allow for the obtaining by way of exchange of any material advantage for the parties or their relations. The State combats in particular the delivery of any consideration or goods by way of *lobolo*, gratification, marriage gift or indemnification [Art. 4].

Although the language of this Article makes it clear that it is not *lobolo* as a whole that is to be combated, but only its commercialized aspect, and although there is nothing to suggest that penal measures should be used in this combat, this Article might well require reformulation, particularly in the light of the findings of the Extraordinary Conference of the Organization of Mozambican Women, to be referred to in the next section. In particular, what should receive more emphasis is that what the state combats is forced marriages, whether of children *lobolo*-ed by their parents, or of widows 'inherited' against their wills by their in-laws according to the rules of *lobolo*. But all forced marriages should be combated, whether associated with *lobolo* or not. Furthermore, to attempt a total demonetarization of marriage might be a bit unrealistic – what needs to be strongly discouraged at the practical level is the subjecting of the groom to extravagant indebtedness arising from his need to find *lobolo*; and what needs to be struggled against at the ideological level is the notion that to be properly married, the bride has to be 'paid for', and that once 'paid for', she 'belongs to' her husband and his family.

On the question of divorce, the Family Law Project follows the practice of the people's tribunals in trying to secure reconciliation and doing everything possible to protect the marriage, but also in not forcing marriages to continue when they are clearly broken down irretrievably. In procedural terms, the Project allows for two types of divorce, divorce by mutual consent after one year's separation, and litigious divorce on the basis of failure of the marriage, due to grievous violation of the rights and duties governing marriage. In practice, the local tribunals were rarely called upon to grant consensual divorces, since where the couples had not registered their marriages the unions created *de facto* (for example, by means of *lobolo* or in Church) could be terminated *de facto*, no question of formal legal status being involved. In cases where the parties could not agree, the local tribunals tended to look to the concrete circumstances of the marriage, whether objectively speaking there was any prospect of keeping it alive, but not to exclude entirely the question of fault. Bearing in mind that men tended to have less need of judicial intervention than did women because they had the power of tradition behind them as well as greater earning power, it can be seen that the local people's tribunals played an important role in protecting the rights of women. In this sense the local tribunals offered an accessible and reliable alternative to dissolution of a marriage according to the rules of *lobolo*, and their experience was consolidated in the Project. As far as the higher courts were concerned, the Family Law Project introduced major reforms, since the Portuguese Civil Code which had still been in force, even though many of its provisions had become void because of unconstitutionality, had basically forbidden divorce in the case of Catholic marriages, and permitted divorce in other cases only on specified and frequently archaic grounds of proven fault. The Family Law Project thus negated both the *lobolo* and the canonic systems, following instead the practice of the local courts, but leaving it open to couples informally to continue to apply the rules of traditional law or the church if they so wished.

From a technical point of view, perhaps the most important feature of the Project was the attention which it gave to the *de facto* union. Instead of being treated as a marginal topic under 'Miscellaneous Provisions' at the end of the Project, *de facto* unions were given extensive treatment in a central section. For purposes of marriage and divorce, *de facto* unions are treated virtually as though they are marriages so that, although constituted differently, their legal effects are virtually the same, and a dissolution of a *de facto* union decreed by the tribunal is roughly equal to a judicial divorce. The generous legal acknowledgement of *de facto* unions thus brings within the terms of the Project the great majority of Mozambican families – estimated at 90% – who have not registered their marriages. It is accordingly an important device for narrowing the gap between registered and unregistered unions and thereby materializing the constitutional principle of treating all citizens alike independently of background. As such it is both democratic in its range and unifying in its operation, as can be seen in relation to its impact on marriages celebrated in terms of the principles of *lobolo*. A *de facto* union is defined as a single relationship between a man and a woman who, being legally capable of marrying, establish between themselves a common life with the serious character of a family and being so regarded by society (Art. 23). The great majority of people married by *lobolo* would fall under this definition, but not those in child marriages or polygamous unions. (Some protection is given to members of polygamous unions when such unions are dissolved – Art. 30.) The payment of *lobolo* does not in itself prove the existence of a *de facto* union, but it has considerable evidential value. Equally, failure to pay *lobolo* would not be decisive in denying the status of a *de facto* union to a situation where the couple clearly lived together as man and wife.

To sum up: (i) most marriages celebrated in terms of *lobolo* would receive an extensive degree of recognition by the courts, not because the *lobolo* was paid but because a union resulted; (ii) the existence of such a union would be legally relevant in relation to impeding further marriage (a member of a *de facto* union has been judicially dissolved), in relation to applying the rules of divorce to the dissolution of the union, and in relation to the attribution of the status of surviving spouse or other beneficiary of such kind; (iii) the normative system relating to *lobolo* would be irrelevant in terms of determining whether such a union existed or should be dissolved, and could not be the basis for claims for damages or specific performance.

The Extraordinary Conference of the Organization of Mozambican Women

Although the Family Law Project underwent many drafts and was the result of many consultations, in the eyes of the Government it failed to respond fully to the cultural dimension of the question. Because of the public importance of the subject, it was felt that a nation-wide discussion should take place on the family and family problems and then the Project be looked at again. Accordingly, certain fundamental aspects of the Project were put into force immediately, namely, those dealing with divorce, *de facto* unions and polygamous unions, but the Project as a whole was suspended (Directive by the President of the High Court Appeal, 27 Feburary 1982).

The task of conducting the nation-wide discussion was given to the Organization of Mozambican Women (OMM). A standard set of themes and questions was elaborated to serve as the basis for discussion in public debate in all ten provinces. Using these questions as a basis, hundreds of mass meetings were held to engage the local population – mainly women but with a good sprinkling of men – in dialogue. Scribes were appointed to record the dominant opinions, bearing in mind that majority and minority views might be expressed. These opinions were then collated on a provincial basis, and finally the provincial reports were integrated into a single final report of the OMM to be presented at the Extraordinary Conference of the Organization. Since the objective was not simply to poll the public, but to involve the public, the mass assembly rather than the random sample became the basic source of information. This allowed for a much more active debate than simple opinion polling would have permitted and also assisted in the capturing of regional and local variations more adequately than random sampling would have made possible.

While the full value of the survey has as yet to be digested, the immediate result was the publication of two documents which served as the basis for the Conference and which continue to serve as the basic guideline for all discussion on topics such as the family and *lobolo*. The first document was the keynote speech, made by President Samora Machel at the beginning of the Conference. Referring to *lobolo*, the President said that it was necessary to identify what *lobolo* represented as a social form for constituting the family, as a means of public recognition of this fact.

> That is to say, it is important for us to understand what *lobolo* contains as an element for establishing a family that is solid, has public prestige and social recognition. We must also know how to distinguish what are the rights over women and mercantile aspects connected with the practice of *lobolo* which challenge the dignity of women . . . The contradictions that exist between the practice of *lobolo* and polygamy, on the one hand, and the emancipation of women on the other, must be resolved by the development of society itself and by the growing consciousness of Mozambican Women.

The second document (OMM, 1983) was prepared by a Central Office especially set up by the OMM for the Conference. It declares that three preliminary points have to be made about traditional marriage:

> First, it was quite natural that the many diverse groups that inhabited the territory of Mozambique should have diverse forms of constituting families.
> Second, these traditional forms of marriage became part of the personality of the people and, at the later stage, part of the cultural resistance to colonialism.
> Third, at the same time, both by virtue of its own tradition and as a result of cultural and socio-economic interference by colonialism, these traditional marriages today are impregnated with elements of exploitation, depersonalization, and psychological inferiorization of women which have nothing to do with the affirmation of the Mozambican personality or even of the African personality.

The struggle that is necessary therefore has two poles: the suppression of the exploitation and humiliation of women by means which include traditional marriage; and the creation of a single civil marriage system which will strengthen national unity and the principle of the equality of all Mozambicans, men and women, before the law.

> Such a single form of marriage, however, recognized by the State in the whole of our country, is not incompatible with the diverse popular cultural and social activities which in each province and each region signify social and family solidarity in relation to the new couple, the new home. On the contrary, such activities belong to our culture and our personality and give to the civil act of matrimony the true cultural dimension of our people. What in truth is necessary is to admit and fully understand that tradition is not necessarily good nor necessarily bad. Everything depends on how the values it carries coordinate with the building of a society of equality and progress, of socialism (OMM, 1983).

Dealing with the principal characteristics of traditional marriage in the southern and central zones of the country, the report says that, although the terminology and the rites might differ, the central aspect is always the transfer of cash in amounts ranging from 3,000 to 100,000 *meticais* (roughly US$75 to US$2,500), consumer goods of great value, ranging from cattle to clothes to radios, etc., in exchange for the movement of the bride from her home to that of the groom.

> Much can be said about the nature of this institution but in our view its character as an immediate exchange, the high spirit of profit (for the bride's parents) implicit in the transaction, means that the expression purchase of the bride is today synonymous with this form of marriage (OMM, 1983).

The man buys the woman; the man exchanges his cattle, his money, his goods, for a wife; the young man works to get money so that he can acquire a wife. The greater her attributes, such as her youth, the social position and prestige of her family, and even her virginity, the more her parents can demand in *lobolo* from the groom. Accordingly, the idea of the marriage as a commercial transaction, of the woman as a thing to buy or sell, is involved in the traditional marriages in these zones: more, it is the central idea. All the rest of the ceremonies, the exchanges of presents, merely accompany the principal aspect which is the transfer of material goods in exchange for the bride.

Dealing with the strategy of struggle which needs to be followed in relation to the negative aspects of the different forms of traditional marriage, the Report states confidently that it is not necessary to convince the people that the exorbitant amounts paid in *lobolo* are negative features which turn the marriage into a business deal. The people know this. It is the men who frequently have to battle to find the means to pay, thus saddling the new home with great financial difficulties. Virtually unanimously, the major proposal we received from the zones in which *lobolo* is practised was to reduce the monetary value of the *lobolo* to 2,500 *meticais* (about US$60). Note that it was frequently men who advanced this proposal.

It will be more difficult, the Report continues, to convince the people that the absence of freedom on the part of women to choose their spouses and the absence of equality in the home of the spouses in relation to each other and in relation to the children, results in a true oppression of women by men, without the ending of which it will never be possible to build a society that is new, more just, economically advanced and free from any form of exploitation.

After stressing that social transformation (especially in the countryside), the involvement of women in production and defence, and active mobilization by the Women's Movement are the keys to overcoming this situation, the Report recommends a number of immediate practical steps such as the 'popularization' of the civil marriage and the creation of mobile brigades of the Registry to record and celebrate marriages.

Finally, it is always necessary to preserve the positive aspects of traditional marriage, such as social and family solidarity with the couple, and abandon the negative aspects such as the humiliation and reification of women as a form of the general struggle for the liberation of women.

Conclusion

Analysing the experience gained in the years since independence, it is possible to say that the strategies which appeared to be inadequate at the time of independence remain inadequate today. Whether or not it will ever be appropriate to attempt to abolish *lobolo*, without very great social, economic, and cultural changes, such a day would be far off indeed. Similarly, to attempt unambiguous conservation or a restoration of *lobolo* in a pure form would not only be reactionary but futile; the institution has suffered irreversible damage from two opposite sides, from the forces of change and revolution on the one side, and from the forces of the market on the other. By the same token, a purely ethnographic or protectionist strategy is out of the question. It is not only that in the present situation an accountant might have more value than an ethnographer, it is that the issue has long been in the public domain and directly affects the courts and the formulation of new legislation in a way that cannot be skirted. The only strategy of those mentioned in the Introduction which may be said to have gained ground is the regulative one. The OMM Extraordinary Conference Report in fact states that the people would readily accept a ceiling being placed on *lobolo*, the amount mentioned being 2,500 *meticais* (approximately US$60).

The regulative strategy would have the advantage of offering a compromise solution in a period of transition. It would indicate that the state does not combat *lobolo* as such, but only the excessive amounts being demanded. The young couple would be the main beneficiaries, in the sense that the groom would not have been forced to mortgage his earnings for years to come, and the bride would only be psychologically indebted in terms of a symbolic price paid for her; moreover, conflicts with the parents would be reduced by having an agreed amount payable and paid.

In the writers' opinion, however, the regulative strategy on its own would be inadequate. While it would have the great virtues of taking some of the unnecessary heat out of the question, and of commanding considerable public support, it raises a number of new issues and leaves many old ones unanswered.

In the first place, as a form of price control, how is it to be implemented without creating a black market (*candonga*) in brides? If parents of the bride continue to insist on presents of great value, how will the State respond? A regulative strategy at most is a starting point for a more profound strategy. The danger is that it will become a pretext for avoiding the more complex strategy altogether. Apart from the cultural and psychological factors involved, there are legal issues to be considered. Should payment or non-payment of lawful amounts of *lobolo* give rise in themselves to the possibility of legal actions? Does the payment of *lobolo* in an amount agreed by the State mean that the State recognizes the whole normative system surrounding *lobolo*, ranging from rights and duties of parties, rights in relation to the children, grounds for divorce, and rights of succession?

What sanctions, if any, should be applied to people who demand or who pay more than the stipulated amounts? Should such people go to prison or be fined? And should excess payments be refundable or forfeit to the state? (And who would report them?) Are multiple *lobolo* payments permissible in the form of polygamy, and what of payment of *lobolo* for child brides, should that too be legitimate, perhaps at half-price?

The careful language used in the OMM Report indicates that the authors were aware of the limitations of the regulatory strategy. In particular, they make it clear that such a strategy by no means diminishes the importance of a concerted struggle against the negative cultural and psychological aspects of *lobolo*. It is true that if the 'price' is a symbolic one and not extremely onerous, the psychological pressure on the bride in its turn becomes symbolic. But symbols can have a vivid life of their own, even if torn from their original material base. The concept that it is the wife's role to serve the husband, a notion intimately bound up with the system of *lobolo*, needs to be tackled head on if women's emancipation is to proceed and the full creative capacity of Mozambican women is to be unleashed.

Firm positions taken in the Report in relation to associated issues such as child marriage and polygamy underline that as far as the OMM is concerned – and in this as in all other important aspects it liaises closely with Frelimo – the mere regulation of the amounts of *lobolo* payments would be far from dealing with the *lobolo* question in its full dimension.

The proposal we make, therefore, is that if regulation of *lobolo* be adopted, it be done not as a strategy in itself, but as part of a wider and more profound strategy, namely, the revolutionary or transformatory strategy.

The revolutionary strategy is characterized by three principal features. It insists that the question of *lobolo* cannot be viewed in a purely abstract or moralistic way shorn of its material base; it insists that the element of time and process is fundamental; and it insists that the main agent of change must be the people themselves.

It is in this context that the words: 'preserve what is good and reject what is bad' cease to be mere platitudes and become a guide to action.

The objective of this study is not to make proposals in relation to all the dimensions of *lobolo*, but to look at the issue in a rounded way so as to make proposals for an appropriate legal strategy. In this connection the following concrete suggestions are made.

First, the negative aspects of *lobolo* should be specifically identified and appropriate actions developed. At the extreme end come child marriages and the 'inheritance' of widows. These should be combated mainly by means of education and persuasion, but the criminal law might be kept in reserve for specially bad cases. Such phenomena could directly be made punishable in certain circumstances (for example, parents pull a 12-year-old girl out of school to marry her off at a good price to a man twice or three times her age). Alternatively, the ordinary principles of the criminal law in relation to consent for sexual relations and kidnapping could be applied. Care should be taken not to prevent widows from voluntarily going to live with their in-laws if this is their wish.

Next would come polygamy. The State should use education and persuasion to combat polygamy, and not think in terms of a regulative strategy as has been adopted in some African countries. The law should not formally recognize polygamous unions, not even as *de facto* marriages, but the law should not at this stage contemplate penal sanctions. Wives in polygamous unions should be assisted by the law if they wish to leave such unions, and in all cases sensible and just provision should be made for children of such unions and for widows or abandoned wives.

In the case of *lobolo* as such, the State should make it clear that it encourages the protocol and feasts of traditional marriages, and that it permits the payments of small sums in terms of tradition, and that provided there would be no impediment in terms of the Civil Law, it recognizes such marriages as producing most of the effects of a civil marriage. In concrete terms this would mean that such marriages could be automatically transcribed by the local 'structures'; that mobile registrars could be created; and that even in the case of non-registration, they would have the standing of the *de facto* unions. Consideration could also be given to a concept of conjugal or matrimonial union which, while starting with civil marriages, would reach out to include marriages by traditional ceremonies and marriages by recognized religious officers. Though for certain purposes the civil marriage might enjoy a privileged position, in general terms the rights and duties of all members of conjugal unions would be the same. Far from diminishing respect for civil marriages, this would ensure that many of the principles of civil marriages would be extended to all marriages. This would be consistent with the present concept of *de facto* unions, but expressed in a way that is more diplomatic. Whereas Jounod in his capacity as missionary posed the question as one of dramatic choice between two ways of life, we prefer to see the issue as one of the transformatory fusions of the best elements of the old and new. The State would also indicate the limits of its support for *lobolo*. It would underline that *lobolo* promises and payments would be regarded purely as matters between the families and not exigible in a court of law. It would affirm clearly that although the parties and families would be free to apply the rules of *lobolo* amongst themselves, they could not invoke the aid of the courts in applying such rules or in enforcing such agreements. Similarly, the State would have to take a position on how it would censure payments which exceeded the stipulated ceiling. On the one hand it could subject the offending people to public criticism, and uphold the rights of the young couple to marry without paying exorbitant amounts. On the other, it could consider civil or penal sanctions against the offenders, preferably of a monetary kind. The difficulties encountered in imposing effective sanctions against those who exceed the regulated prices of foodstuffs suggest, however, that a purely administrative or penal approach to matters essentially of an economic (and, here, of a cultural) nature, has little effect save to bring the law into disrepute.

Finally, the State could use the resources under its control to encourage young women to continue their education, to be integrated into the economy, and to be active in the defence of the country. It could enlarge the network of crêches and expand the provision of meals for workers. It could continue its support for women's co-operatives and for the development of communal villages. It could maintain its position that schoolbooks, media programmes, and cultural activity promote the constitutional principle of equality.

If the liberation of women is a pre-condition for the advance of the revolution, so is the general advance of the revolution a necessity for the liberation of women.

Notes

1. Interviews with Raul Honwana, former court interpreter, 77 years old, and his wife Naly Nhaca, 62 years old, housewife, member of the Organization of Mozambique Women, conducted on 6, 10 and 14 May 1982.

6. The Two Dimensions of Socialist Legality: Recent Experience in Mozambique*

As a contribution to the debate I would like to offer a few informal and hastily prepared observations which, I should stress, represent personal opinions only. It's interesting to observe that when things are going well in Mozambique as far as the legal system is concerned, we speak about 'popular justice', and that when we have problems, we speak about 'socialist legality'. We don't speak all that often about socialist legality[1] – it doesn't crop up except when it has to be 'reinforced'; and what I'm going to refer to today is the two sets of circumstances that have arisen since I've been in Mozambique, in which it's been found necessary to 'reinforce socialist legality'. I think it's not accidental that it's been these two, because I think they represent the two facets, the two interconnected aspects of socialist legality which because of the open, underdeveloped and rapidly developing nature of Mozambican society – perhaps because of some of the specific features of the Mozambican revolution – come out in very clear forms. You can see the bones, they're not hidden under a thick skin of public relations. Therefore I will speak in terms of these two concrete experiences.

I'll start with an experience of a few months ago. We were playing bridge one evening, myself and some friends whom I jokingly call relics of the old colonial bourgeoisie, who have identified, as they would call it, with the revolutionary process. I don't know if it's a lapse or if it's a legitimate pastime, but once a week we get together to play bridge, and there were seven of us – and for those of you who play bridge, you'll know seven is the worst number because you have one table complete plus three impatient people waiting for the eighth person to arrive – and it was at half past eight he should have been there, nine o'clock he should have been there, nine-thirty he rolled up. And instead of coming up with the usual kinds of apologies, which are normally that there had been an emergency – he's a doctor – he just said 'I was listening to the radio', and he'd been listening to a speech by Samora Machel, who is the President of the country, the President of Frelimo, and he said 'Samora was fantastic, he was brilliant, oh he gave it to them!' And so we're dealing out the cards, asking:

* Transcript of a talk given by Albie Sachs to the International Sociological Association Research Committee on the Sociology of Law workgroup on 'Beyond Formal Justice', Antwerp, 1983, and published earlier in the *International Journal of the Sociology of Law*, London, Vol. 13, No. 2, 1985.

'Well what did he say?' and we're bidding 'one no trump, two clubs' and so on. 'Oh he gave it to them, he really gave it to them, it was fantastic!' I said 'But gave it to whom?' 'He gave it to them, he closed down the Law Faculty.'

And that was the first information I had that I was about to be out of a job. This was a speech that the President was making to the delegates at the Popular Assembly, dealing with a whole range of issues, and he was 'giving it to them', that is, it was a speech criticizing the institutions that Frelimo itself had created, criticizing the personnel working in those institutions, criticizing the state structure if you like, in a very severe way; and what was the final nail in our coffin, apparently, was that the biggest applause that he got in a long and very punchy and very spirited speech, came when he said '. . . and from tomorrow [or next week or whenever it was] the Law Faculty will be closed'. We had to think about that, we still have to think about that, not only why it was found necessary to close the Law Faculty, but why people applaud attacks on lawyers so much. What did the Law Faculty represent to the delegates that they thought this was a good thing, that this was dealing with something that's going wrong in terms of the revolutionary process, something inimical to the welfare of the people?

This was the first salvo in a series of shots that caused a lot of turbulence in the whole justice sector – a turbulence from which many have not fully recovered even now. New legislation was introduced, which for the first time since independence imposed whipping as a method of punishment to be used in particular cases, and subsequent to that came examples of public flogging in different parts of Mozambique. And this was done in a way which was given maximum publicity, it wasn't something done behind closed doors, something done and denied, which happens in many countries – it was almost the reverse of the situation in other countries where violence is used but is officially denied. Here it was officially being proclaimed, and proclaimed from the rooftops, that we are going to whip people, and we're going to whip people in public. Some persons remarked sadly in private, 'The first lash fell on my shoulders'. Clearly, the whipping law came as a shock to many who had been inspired over the years by the humanist traditions of the Mozambican revolution. For example, the question of how to treat captured Portuguese soldiers had cropped up as a very pertinent issue right at the beginning of the liberation war, and one group inside Frelimo said, 'They're white oppressors and they've come to shoot us and kill us and torture us and massacre us, and we will kill them', and the other group said:

> But who are these people? They are children of peasants in Portugal, themselves victims of fascist oppression, they are disarmed now, they are in our power – and we must re-educate them, we mustn't kill them, we must show them who we are, what we are fighting for, the justice of our cause, so that they can then go back to their own country and participate in the liberation struggle of their own country as well,

and that was a real, concrete issue that split Frelimo at that stage, and

Samora Machel and others representing the revolutionary and humanist current were victorious and every single captured Portuguese soldier was alive at the end of the war and was handed over, though not a single captured Frelimo soldier survived, they were all killed, usually after torture. And the line was: 'We don't take our morality from the enemy, we create our own morality, a morality of liberation'. There were other issues that also cropped up long before independence: the question of whether women should participate in the armed struggle, and Josina Machel said, 'Why can't *I* fight for the liberation of my people, why should I be excluded because I'm female?' and the same people who wanted to shoot the captured Portuguese soldiers answered, 'But how can we have women in the army, they don't know how to fight?' and she and the others said, 'Of course we don't know how to fight, we haven't been trained, how can we know how to fight if we're not trained? Give us the training and we will fight alongside the men as patriots of our country'. And then these men insisted, 'Even if you learnt how to fight, what will our people say? That Frelimo is so weak and so desperate that it's giving guns to women', and then Josina and Samora and the others said:

> Well, if our people say that, our people are backward in this respect, and part of the revolutionary process is to transform the outlook, the mentality of our people, to liberate the creative forces of our people, and to overcome the whole dead weight of traditional feudalism that's keeping our people in bondage and facilitating the colonial domination of our people.

There are many more examples, not of pious declarations but of concrete positions adopted during the armed struggle: the whole concept of health as hygiene, that people have responsibility for themselves, for their bodies, they learn how to keep themselves healthy, and they're not dependent on prescriptions from doctors, which they didn't have anyhow, and health is really a question of boiling the water, of keeping yourself clean, of eating well, and health is something that people must acquire for themselves, and not get as some kind of benefit from specialists. And in the case of education, they closed down – this is a precedent for closing down the Law Faculty – they closed down the Mozambican Institute in Dar-es-Salaam in the mid-1960s, because the students were refusing to go to the liberated zones during the war, arguing: 'If we go there, and we participate in literacy programmes, and in general transformation of society there, we're putting ourselves at risk, we might be killed, and after all we are the future teachers and lawyers and engineers for Mozambique, and we are too valuable to go there, let others go there and do the fighting'. And the Frelimo leaders said, 'Well, if our school is producing people like that, we would rather have no school at all, because that's not what the revolution is about, and not what education is about'. I mention these themes to stress that the humanist, popular tradition is indeed part and parcel of the very character of the Mozambican revolution. And the present leadership was formed in the course of those struggles. They were good military commanders – but they were not just that. They included brilliant orators, but they didn't become leaders because of that. They became leaders because during this phase of fierce internal struggle – what they call the great contradictions, the crisis that hit the national liberation movement before independence, they were the people who adopted what was called the revolutionary line, the internationalist line, the line that the objective of the struggle was not to expel the Portuguese so that they could take over exploitation from them – the objective was to destroy exploitation in all forms; and that included traditional forms of exploitation, which of course was very important in the African context.

And so that's the background against which we have to evaluate these latest measures. In other words, these were decisions taken at a specific stage in the struggle to serve particular purposes. They were not reflections of a tradition of thinking that you can eliminate social evils simply by means of the rod.

Returning to the theme of socialist legality as it emerged earlier this year, we have to ask why and how it came to be projected in such a severe form. The why emerged piece by piece – there wasn't one simple statement about why whipping had been introduced. It came out in blocks of information, and a lot of informal observations that we received. But the background was very very clear in generalized terms – the background is simply one of revolution and counter-revolution. And counter-revolution in the Mozambican context takes the form of international conflict. At the time of independence in 1975, the old what they called colonial bourgeoisie fled to South Africa and Rhodesia, expecting to be able to storm their way back within months, and they had all sorts of plans ready. When they were unable to come back within months, they associated themselves first with the Smith regime, and then with the apartheid regime in South Africa. And in effect, they became instruments of foreign regimes and organizations rather than indigenously-based counter-revolutionary, or anti-revolutionary, or whatever-you-might-like-to-call-them forces. It gave them a certain strength, it also gave them a great weakness. The strength was the backing of a foreign state. The weakness was that they lost their roots inside the country, and very few patriots would even think of supporting them; they were openly identified with forces hostile to Mozambican independence and that became their medium- and long-term weakness. In addition, their particularly brutal and non-political mode of operation strengthened the conviction that they were operating as instruments of others rather than as discontented patriots. This was counter-revolution as a reality and it assumed two fundamental forms: the one was the armed groups that were coming in from camps in the north-eastern Transvaal and northern Natal, and attacking villages, attacking co-operative farms, attacking the transport communications, and providing a cover for South African-trained military commandos of foreign states to come in and blow up petrol tank depots, bridges, economic targets that were important, not only to the economy of Mozambique but to the economy of Zimbabwe and to the integration of SADCC as were called the zone countries seeking to create an alternative economic unit in southern Africa, independent and relatively free of South Africa.

So that was the physical, direct physical form that counter-revolution took, and it was serious, and it was extensive in the whole of the centre part of the country and it held back not only economic development, but the whole capacity of the leadership to concentrate on social problems, on educational problems, the problems of chronic underdevelopment. If all the time you're having to think about the military threat, it just leaves very little over for developing a planned economy, developing economic resources. But this was only one of the threats, and this wasn't the threat that was responsible for the whipping law, though it was part of the general background. The other threat was the attempt to strangle the food supply; it was the growing black market, the means of manipulating a general shortage of food partly caused by the armed attacks, but not simply caused by that, in order to create popular discontent, to create a climate in which it would be easy for the regime to be overthrown. And there of course one sees a very clear analogue of the situation, say in Chile in 1973, where it was the armed forces that struck the blow and destroyed the new power of the popular unity government, but they did so in a climate that had been created of a certain popular unease and dislocation, directly linked with the strike of the truckers and the lack of food in the towns. And so the banging of empty pots and pans by middle-class housewives became the symbol of counter-revolution at that stage. And as the present Mozambican Minister of Justice said once:

> counter-revolution is a science, it's not simply a series of empirical actions to bring about a change in a country, it's not simply a bit of plotting done by a few, highly-skilled personnel with their chosen people in the country whose government they're trying to overthrow – it's a global, total strategy that operates on the military front, on the psychological front, the cultural front, and very much on the food front.

And to deal with it, you have to deal with it also in this global kind of way.

With state power at the command of counter-revolution, coupled with its capacity to link up with various international economic organizations, it was possible to subject a country like Mozambique to a concerted, scientifically-planned form of siege, with the object of slowly strangling and then rapidly overthrowing the revolution. Overthrowing the revolution doesn't mean placing nice, democratic people in power who will then say, 'Okay, chaps, we're going to have freedom of this, and freedom of that and the other'. It will mean killing off all those who've been basically associated with the new power, the Machelistas as they call them, as is happening even now in the rural areas.

We visited a number of rural co-operatives in which, when these armed bands came in, they said, 'Who's the chairman of the co-operative?' and they just cut at him in the stomach with a bayonet and he was dead. 'Who's the secretary of the women's movement?' and they cut off her nose and ears and breasts, and said 'Now you go out and show the world who's got power in this country', and it's at that level of physical brutality that the question of counter-revolution is being posed, and one knows what they will do if they were to succeed, these were people who were trained in the commandos in colonial times – they went round burning – that's blacks alienated from their own people – burning black villages and killing and massacring, they stop buses now and they shoot up the passengers. It's a very harsh kind of situation, that in which our debates are conducted. As far as the towns are concerned, the big problem is food, and the distribution of food. And the reason why – indirectly – the Law Faculty was closed, was because of food.

This year Frelimo had its second general congress since independence, and it was a congress essentially of re-evaluation, of scaling down on the programme, on their objectives, and of a deep analysis of why so many things were going wrong. Perhaps the most important part of the congress was the run-up period of about a year that preceded the congress. They published something like twelve, what they called, theses – very generalized, rather abstract statements, on the economy, on international relations, on culture, on security and so on. And these were taken to the people, as platforms for debate and discussion, in all the areas where you had organized community life. It could be in the ministries, or in factories or in farms, it could be in an area where people were living together – in a rural area – wherever it might be. And the people discussed, under the headings of these theses, what was going wrong in their particular sector, and the objective was to make the discussion as concrete as possible. What was going wrong, and who's responsible for it, were the two big things. And it seems that teams that went around and had to collate all this information got one set of answers throughout the country that was expressed with more vehemence than any other, and universally – and that was the question of black marketeering. This was something that injured the people not simply in their bodies but in their souls, and the line was:

> We know that we are a poor country, we know that we have many difficulties, that we're inexperienced, and we make mistakes through inexperience. We know that we are trying new things, and when you try new things you make lots of mistakes, and we are willing to put up with hardships, and we know that we have outside forces squeezing us and creating problems for us – that we know, and we're not complaining about the hardships, but what we cannot tolerate is the fact that there are some people who are parasitic, who are benefiting, who are living well, and who are laughing at our hardships, and that we can't take.

This is a very local and a very real thing. You know that round the corner, living next door, is X, and in the backyard of his rather humble reed hut he's got six sacks of rice, and four of sugar, and these have been stolen from somewhere. And he's selling that to his friends or to anybody, at four or five times or ten times the stipulated price.

> 'And whenever we try to do something about it', the people complained, 'nothing happens. We call in the police, the police come along, he's arrested, and the next day he's back in his house. He's out on bail they tell us, and he's still selling these things. It makes no difference. Or he goes to jail, and he seems to come out of jail as often as he's in it, or he might be in jail for three months and he comes back and he's still doing the same kind of thing. And what's the Frelimo doing? Where's your power? You say you're in

> power, you're speaking about power all the time, and nothing happens – and this black market is growing, it's getting worse and worse, and we can't stand it, and you must do something about it.' When asked what, the people said, 'You must beat them, and beat them in front of everybody so that everybody knows what's going on'.

And here you have a dilemma. We want law to be democratic, we want to be responsive to the people, to the people's needs and demands. The people are not speaking in a lynch-mob kind of atmosphere – this is a serious, calm kind of discussion. They are dealing with very concrete, very real problems, and they are saying that if you don't do this, you might have your beautiful, pure revolution, but you're going to lose – there's going to be discontent, and the enemy is going to walk in, because they're going to be able to solve the food problem better than you. What do you do? Do you respond to the sovereignty of the people? It's a complicated question. Frequently in the past the Mozambican leaders have stressed that you don't simply expect the right results to come automatically from the voice of the people, this is sheer populism. You have to be involved in a relationship with the people; the theme of leadership comes in, of transformation, or revolution, of evolving a new consciousness. That implies that you're engaging with the people and combating many of the old ideas and attitudes of the people.

On the other hand, one must listen to the people, these are understandable demands from the people, and why do we have such a violent objection to whipping? Is it part of our own cultural formation, heavily influenced by rather generalized international ideas about what's possible or what's not? It's possible to bomb, drop atom bombs, and to blow up people and to let them live in ghettos and to humiliate them in all sorts of ways, but to hit them with the whip is regarded as something particularly uncivilized and barbaric. Do we allow our criteria to be established by the editorial writers of the world, or do we rather listen to what our people are saying, the ones who have to stand in the queues for food, the ones who have to suffer the hardships of hunger, do we rather listen to them and respond in the cultural form that has meaning to them and is appropriate to what they want?

In this way, to the extent that there's an attempt to theorize this, although it's much more a question not so much of theorizing as of finding measures that are regarded as appropriate at a certain stage – what is said is that what we're witnessing in Mozambique is 'a failure of socialist legality'. Legality in this context means that the people feel confident that the law is there to protect their interests, to protect their rights and if, under the guise of granting bail, under the guise of a re-education programme in which people walk in and out of the prisons, the result is that people lose respect for the legal system – the people feel that it's not protecting them, it's protecting the parasites, it's protecting the crooks and the black marketeers, it's protecting the people who'd be only too happy if apartheid came to their country, then there is no legality, there is an absence of legality.

Legality is the organized way in which the state protects the people as a whole, defends them against aggression and against exploiters and black-marketeers, and what the people were saying was that one of the reasons for the failure of legality was that those in the courts, in charge of dealing with these problems, were so out of touch with the popular mood, were so out of touch with the anxieties and the passions and the feelings and the thoughts of the people living in these very poor areas, the people who really are the bastion and the main support of the revolution, that they were simply following the old codes in an automatic way, feeling very virtuous in doing that, feeling very progressive to grant bail, because they were still mentally colonized by the formulae, by the ideas, by the values of the past – values that in the struggle against fascism in Portugal had had a definite meaning, but values totally out of phase with the needs of the revolutionary process in Mozambique. And they asked why it was that the judges were so out of touch:

> they're our judges, produced by our Law Faculty, created after independence, they are Mozambicans, we can't point a finger to anybody else, we can't put the blame on anybody else, and we can't say well, these are Portuguese expatriates imposing their values on us; they're our people.

And the answer was that there was something wrong in the kind of legal education that was being given in the Law Faculty. This had already been noted in the ministries – many lawyers were coming out ineffective, they couldn't write out contracts, they couldn't handle problems of internal discipline, they couldn't deal with international trade, they couldn't create a robust, new kind of legal precedent that corresponded to the needs of the new society. And they would frequently make up for their practical incompetence with a certain arrogance: if our society doesn't correspond to our legal ideas and our notions, so much the worse for our society, it's underdeveloped, and backward. Instead of saying, 'Our legal ideas are inappropriate, they're a legacy of the past, and we have to adapt our legal ideas to the dynamic of the revolution, which is rich and creative and innovative', their attitude would be just the opposite. So there was the sense of dysfunction, of jarring, which reflected itself in the tremendous applause in the Popular Assembly, that somehow many of the law graduates represented something which was felt to be tainting the whole revolutionary process – these relatively privileged people who had never taken part in the revolution, who had been its main beneficiaries in material terms, who were now living in the beautiful apartments vacated by the colonial bourgeoisie, who were now, some of them, driving around in cars, or were being driven to work in cars, who would know all the correct terminology to use, who would know how to dress, when to stand up, when to sit down, and how to write out beautiful letters and to write reports – and there's nobody can write reports like the Mozambicans – but who in fact contributed nothing, produced nothing, while the people sweated. They were just empty. They were a kind of perpetuation in the revolutionary society of those rather feeble functionaries of the colonial society. And so the applause was saying:

> We know what they're like, we know that they are full of empty knowledge

> and big phrases, and they are representing certain class positions and class attitudes that are actually acting as a brake on the revolutionary process, and that's why we cheer when the Law Faculty is being closed down.

People didn't know the Law Faculty as such, they didn't know what was being taught there, but they knew what many of the products symbolized, and, even if some graduates have made outstanding contributions to the revolution, while others have conducted themselves correctly and competently as patriots of the country, far too many conformed to the figure of emptiness and arrogance.

Well, the adoption of the whipping law, apart from issues it raises in itself, raises an aspect of socialist legality that in some ways makes us all uncomfortable, because it stresses the fact that socialist legality means repression, repression that represses, that doesn't just talk about repression, that has teeth, that hurts those people who are seen as destroying the gains that have been made after heavy sacrifice by generations to achieve independence and social advance. And perhaps I can illustrate the kind of lack of contact, even after the Presidential statement had been made, even after the reasons had been given in Parliament for discontent with the products of the Law Faculty and the whole town was buzzing about this (even our bridge game was held up because of this!!). One of the judges – and these are all friends, that we know, and like, it's not just somebody over there, somebody you read about – had a case in one of the higher criminal courts. A train driver used to arrive at a village near the Swazi border, and give three toots on his whistle – you know, these old trains still in service, these real '*chook-chook*' steam trains – 'toot toot toot', and the villagers would come out, and they would know that this was the signal to buy stolen rice. So he and the guards were all in on this scheme. Now in this climate of shortages, of hunger, a climate in which people queued, people had rations to get an equal amount for everybody – to behave like that is not only a violation of the job as a train driver – and everybody somehow thinks of locomotive drivers as being particularly moral or noble – it's theft of public goods, of food destined for the people. He'd been doing this over a long period of time, everybody knew about it in the vicinity, it was a public scandal, and it was a severe challenge for the authority of the new power. And what the judge said (and it wasn't even the first time, it was the second time the driver had been charged) was to the effect:

> You've got a wife, you've got four children, and you don't earn very much, and it's no good sending you to jail for a long period because people don't get reformed in jail, therefore, I'm going to give you a suspended sentence.

Well, maybe it was a three-month actual sentence, or six months. She was absolutely out of touch with the whole debate going on in the country, these immense themes that represented either the continuation of the new power, or a return to the old, there was no in-between in the concrete situation. The conclusion was drawn that here was a group of people in the courts existing in their own little autonomous sphere, applying a set of principles and rules that were vaguely progressive as against the Portuguese colonial fascist kind of ideology, but absolutely out of phase with the revolutionary process, problems of hunger and the fight against it.

Another example, less dramatic, but equally revealing, was given to me by one of the more innovative generation of judges. He was the Judge President of the court in Maputo, quite an important court, and once he heard a case of two partners in a garden plot outside Maputo, one of the partners alleging that the other was filching stuff to use on his own plot which his wife was operating a few miles away, stealing implements, fertilizer, even some of the produce. The lawyer who appeared for the defence stood up, and with a finger pointing to the ceiling, would say in a pompous voice, 'And if we look to the illustrious works of Professor So-and-So of Coimbra University, and we examine in profundity the concept of possession, we will see that . . . and we will find our arguments strengthened' and then he would use the finger on the other hand, also pointing to the ceiling, 'If you refer to the esteemed Professor So-and-So of Lisbon University, also dealing with this very complex concept of possession . . .'. This was specious argument, totally invented and irrelevant, gleaned from notes from the Law Faculty, in a show put on for the client to be like one of the lawyers of old. The issue was in reality a common sense one. Was he stealing or wasn't he stealing, was the behaviour dishonest or wasn't it dishonest? Very robust practical questions – is this transgressing the norms of relationships between partners operating here and now in the Green Belt outside Maputo? All that fanciful kind of disputation, quoting refined legal dogmatics, was actually a barrier to arriving at a just result. So these were some concrete illustrations of how out of touch with reality the court atmosphere could be even with new young judges and lawyers in revolutionary Mozambique.

This was a gloomy period, as you can imagine, for many people. We don't like to face up to the repressive element in legality, and one of the reasons we don't like to is partly that those of us who've grown up in capitalist countries, know that the repression is against the poor, it's against the people, it's to some extent against women, it's against the various groups that are oppressed and marginalized. And so we develop habits of mind of being anti-state, anti-authority, because when the state and authority operate, we know it's against causes, against people, against things that we are supporting. So partly it's a habit of mind, it's almost a culture of opposition to authority that we're involved in. But obviously it's not only that – it's an awareness of the crimes that have been committed in socialist countries in the name of defending the revolution. And I don't think there's a country that's completely escaped it – and so it's a sensitivity to that, to the false confessions, to the unjustified purges, to the arbitrary repressions that have taken place as documented in the Soviet Union's Twentieth Socialist Congress Report which spoke about violations of socialist legality associated with the cult of the personality, and China, after the overthrow of the so-called 'Gang of Four' – again there was extensive literature on the theme of socialist legality and reports of abuse of socialist legality.

Well, the theme that took over afterwards was the more positive one – you must grow more food, our leaders must go out to the countryside, they must live amongst the people, we must overcome this undue centralism whereby everything is done by means of a paper sent from an office – and the thrust now is not on the repressive aspects, the thrust now is on encouraging the creative initiative of the people, and various mechanisms have been introduced to achieve that. I contrast this period of the shouting from the rooftops, trumpeting from the rooftops the repressive aspects – that the revolution will defend itself, that the revolution has teeth and will bare them publicly so that people can see them – with the other aspect of legality and the other occasion on which considerable reference was made to the importance of socialist legality. That was in November 1981, and the President acting, as he said in his constitutional role, as guarantor of the rights of the citizens, convened a mass public meeting in the Independence Square, in the centre of Maputo, to speak on the question of abuse of citizens' rights and violations of socialist legality. He gave many examples, ranging from prisoners being assaulted, to cases taking months and years to come to the courts, to people using their uniforms to get to the head of the queue, and certainly those of you who are British would know what a violation of the social norms it is to jump the queue – a whole variety of concrete examples he gave like that, of ways in which power was being abused by people acting in the name of power? And he posed the question: 'How does this happen? We fought for justice, and we find injustice in our country, how does this happen? Who's responsible for it, and why?' The reasons that he gave were concrete ones, and much less juridically-oriented than many lawyers would think appropriate. He said the real problem lay in the nature of the people who came into the police force, the kind of training that they get and the relationships that they had with the community. The solution, then, wasn't so much in new laws and procedural checks and controls (although he said that one reason why we get these abuses is that we are still lumbered with the whole panoply of colonial-type laws that are remote from the people, so that a precondition for achieving true legality is to destroy the old colonial codes and to create a new set, a new kind of legislation that's more open, that's more accessible and more responsive to the needs of the people — the revolution needs law, it needs legislation and due process, it needs courts and lawyers, but these need to be of a new type, oriented to the people, with a new style, language and ethics), but the primary thing was control of the police, he said. The police were not people who had taken part in the liberation struggle, they were mainly people from the towns, from the south, who had not been involved in the big upheavals and the main revolutionary processes which had taken place in the liberated zones in the north. And there had been too much emphasis on technical training and not enough on general cultural transformation and the general outlook of the police. And their relationship with the people was an incorrect one; and from then on, as a directive, every community had to have a neighbourhood form of control over the police, and the police had to be answerable to the community. And that was seen as the most fundamental mechanism of preventing abuses of power.

Privately, the President let it be known to journalists that the position of the country was a difficult one, with imperialism and racism breathing down its neck, and the only way to survive was with the support of the people – 'If we create a police state, we won't have the support of the people, and the racists will be able to walk in'. So it wasn't simply seen as a moral question, a question of what's right, it was also a question of surviving, either by terror or by means of popular support.

> In the end it's popular support that's the only guarantee of the survival of the revolution. And for that reason we have to control ourselves, the state that we've created, our own mechanisms, our own institutions, we have to control them so that the people will then feel these are theirs.

The meeting on legality called by the President was followed by a few weeks which I found quite amusing, where reporters were going around stopping people on the streets and asking them 'Have you heard of any abuses of power?' And the people were coming up with some story, 'Well, my cousin went to the police station, and they kept him there for 72 hours . . .'. 'Oh that's nothing, I mean anything really terrible . . .'. And the whole line was to now look around for terrible things that had happened, that could be exposed. And so the whole thrust of socialist legality at that stage was to expose abuses and to make people acting in the name of the public power answerable to the community, to the power, to the government, to the party.

So there you see, in what was a very Mozambican way, through public meetings, public statements, not coming from lawyers but coming from the President, coming from the main representative of the public power in terms of political statements and not of socio-legal statements, not of conferences of small specialist groups but in terms of a lead given to the whole society – you see these two aspects of socialist legality entering into public life in dramatic forms, visibly, even violently. Clearly, in theoretical terms, there's no incompatibility between the two. On the contrary, the one presupposes the other. If you don't defend the revolution, and it's under attack in physical forms and economic forms, there can't be any upholding of the rights of the people. On the other hand, if the people don't feel that the revolution is theirs, and that the power is theirs, and the governing party is theirs, or their instrument, that the police force is theirs, that the army is theirs, that the law is theirs, then what are you defending? You're simply defending power as power, power as a form of institutional organization, and not people's power, and you're confusing the two. So ideally there should be a dialectical relationship between the two, each reinforcing the other and strengthening the other. In practice it doesn't work that way. In practice, at any particular stage, a need becomes 'claimant' as they said, claiming, demanding the publication and dramatization of either the one aspect or the other aspect. And the dialectical relationship, over a period of time, takes the form of an opposition to the other, as it were. And this is what we've lived through over the past three years, an almost violent opposition of the theme on the one hand, of controlling abusive power, creating mechanisms and a culture in which the people feel free, and are organized so as to control the power that acts in their name, and the effective exercise of power on the other hand.

I would say on the basis of our limited experience that somehow this is an experience that all revolutionary processes necessarily undergo, even if in very different ways – that both these themes inevitably manifest themselves at different stages. The fundamental problem then, is to find the ways of articulating the correct relationship between controls of abuse of power on the one hand, and the effective exercise of power on the other hand – that this is the crucial problem of socialist legality, that the country, the leadership, the government, the people, the courts, the lawyers, the law school have to face up to, analyse, study, experience and overcome. And I think one of the things we find is that the experience in other countries that have undergone revolutionary transformations is interesting, it's valuable, it needs to be studied and evaluated, but in relation to concrete questions, it's not all that helpful. You have to look to the guts of your own society, to the cultural modes, the historical traditions, the ways of saying and doing things that have emerged in the course of a long period of political struggle, and if revolution means anything, it means a struggle involving millions, not just a little culture that's been developed by an elite, by theoreticians living on the margins of the revolutionary society. Never straying from the framework of general theory that is universal (but because it's universal it's sometimes so general as to not be very helpful in concrete situations) and on the basis of a concrete study of the concrete cultural and historical context in which your struggle has evolved, and your political and state forms emerged, you have to try to find your concrete way forward.

I've left out the whole theme of popular justice, that's the bright side, when things are going well. I haven't spoken about the way we helped the people to establish courts in the villages, the way they're functioning. All I can say, without justifying my statement but confident of its truth, is that the new popular tribunals, running into their hundreds, are amongst the most positive gains, as they call it, of the revolution. The people solve their problems, applying progressive new kinds of norms, and it's the people themselves, organized, that do this, they express a power when they do that, they're not controlling power, they're expressing power, and they achieve a very large degree of involvement and support from the community in general. I merely mention it as a very rich experience, and a wonderful one for a lawyer wishing to see justice transformed into a true instrument of community expression. The theme that dominated my presentation is the harder and often less joyous one that has been forced by vivid and at times violent events into our consciousness, the crucially important theme for any revolutionary society, since it deals directly with the meaning of power for the people, the theme of how concretely at any stage to articulate the principles of socialist legality. The struggle continues, and the debate continues too.

Notes

1. Since the talk was given, the question of socialist legality has come very much to the fore in Mozambique, and is frequently referred to.

7. Beyond Pluralism: The Mozambican Experience*

The debate on the question of imposed law versus indigenous law in Africa has been going on for many years and does not seem to be making much progress. One reason, in our view, is that the problem is invariably put in a way that is far too limited, reducing the issue to a simple one of so-called western law versus so-called customary law. An interesting feature of the discussion is that progressive lawyers tend to divide on the subject, those in Africa tending to be rather more impatient of traditional law and procedures than those abroad.

Our experience in Mozambique of attempting to construct a legal order based on community-controlled courts suggests that the options are wider than the imposed/indigenous antinomy presupposes, and that legal pluralism is not the only mechanism for ensuring a people-centred legal order.

We now have more than ten years' experience of trying to build a legal system based on the principles of popular justice. We are aware that this is a term that arouses strong emotions amongst lawyers, and that even to get a hearing on the subject it is sometimes necessary to use other terminology (grassroots-based; community-controlled). Whatever significance popular justice might have for others, however, we in Mozambique judge it in relation to its role in the struggle for independence and for the consolidation of nationhood. For us,the criteria whereby popular justice should be judged are:

- to what extent the people are directly and on a large scale involved in the general formulation and implementation of the law, ensuring that it is sensitive to their wishes;
- to what extent the creative capacity of the people is utilized in the search for solutions to concrete problems of dispute and conflict;
- to what extent the consciousness and behaviour of the people are transformed in the course of their being active agents in the process of exercising judicial authority and solving their own problems.

Applying these criteria rather than the more abstract or formal ones normally put forward by lawyers, we feel that we in Mozambique can point to many successes, as we can refer to an equally large number of failures. The failures

* This paper was originally presented by Gita Honwana Welch to a *Conference on Legal Pluralism and Ethnicity*, Nairobi, Kenya, 1985.

are, of course, often more interesting than the successes, and certainly need to be analysed with great seriousness. Yet, whatever the final verdict will be, and in the last resort the analysis that counts is the analysis that the people themselves make, we are confident that the establishment of popular tribunals in the communities based on principles of equal justice will be considered one of the most innovative and rewarding achievements of the post-independence era.

Mozambique, as with other sub-Saharan countries, was settled by Bantu people after the great migrations which our continent saw over the last thousand years. More recently, at the beginning of the 19th century, a Zulu migration began which resulted in further settlement in the southern part of our country.

The northern coast also witnessed a strong Arab–Muslim influence which from about the tenth century expanded into the interior towards Lake Niassa. Added to all these factors came Portuguese colonial penetration, first along the coast, and then at the end of the last century into the interior.

The result of all this is that Mozambique presents a complex linguistic, cultural and racial picture. At least twenty national languages are spoken, not to speak of countless dialects. Even though (excluding Portuguese) all share Bantu roots, each has its own grammatical and etymological characteristics. Thus we may refer to the principal linguistic–cultural groups as being the Maraves (including the languages Nyanja, Swahili, Ajava, Macua, Makonde) to be found principally in the northern provinces of Niassa, Cabo Delgado, Nampula and Zambezia; the Chuabos, in the southern part of Zambezia; the Tswara in the north-east of Tete Province; the Nguni, Nyungwe and Shona in parts of Tete; Manica and Sofala in the centre of the country; the Sena in Sofala; and finally, the Tsonga in the southern provinces of Inhambane, Gaza and Maputo. Each province on its own and all the provinces together have to be considered as mosaics.

Before colonial penetration each linguistic–cultural group had its own forms of social organization, its own forms of art, crafts and culture, its specific forms of production and distribution, its own social structure and values; even if each in turn was the result of previous epochs of acculturation.

Portuguese colonialism, which for five centuries exploited and oppressed the mosaic of peoples of what today is the People's Republic of Mozambique, constituted a particularly atrocious form of colonialism because of the great cultural underdevelopment and backwardness of the productive forces in Portugal itself, in comparison with other European colonial powers. (We may add that a large part of the Portuguese population was subjected to brutal repression by the same backward regime, and fought courageously for their rights as we fought for ours.)

At the level of law and the administration of justice, the discriminatory practices of Portuguese colonialism in Mozambique translated themselves into a dualist legal system that, far from having the objective of conferring special rights on the 'natives', was designed to give to the colonialists the same rights as their compatriots enjoyed in the metropole, while conserving and enlarging sources of cheap labour in the colony, thereby furthering the economic interests of colonialism.

This is to say that as far as we Mozambicans are concerned, any form of pluralism inevitably meant subtle or not so subtle forms of discrimination between various persons, within the context of a legalized and institutionalized status based on racial or ethnic origin, religious persuasion or social position.

The concern expressed by Portuguese colonialism 'not to shock the native mentality nor to impose on the native a foreign culture, but rather to give him complete freedom of action within the framework of his own institutions, gradually introducing him into the habits of the civilized', was a weak pretext to justify profound racial and social segregation and economic exploitation, as the following account based on interviews and library research proves.

The Dualist Legal System of Colonial Times

The above account establishes that the legal system throughout this period was characterized essentially by the existence of one set of laws for the colonists and another for the 'natives'. In respect of civil law, traditional or religious legal rules were supposed to be applicable to the 'natives'. Yet in the eyes of the colonialists, these local laws never rose above the status of mere uses and customs, which were either ignored by the administrators when inconvenient (for example, when the colonists wished to dispossess the people of land) or else merely tolerated when they did not go contrary to the so-called dictates of humanity and Christian civilization.

For us Mozambicans, therefore, pluralism – defined as the interaction of two or more legal systems within a single state – cannot be separated from Portuguese colonial oppression and its legacy. In fact, the pluralist relationship meant a relationship of subordination and domination. Traditional precolonial law was tolerated to a certain degree, but in a distorted form and only to the extent that it did not inconvenience the colonists. Its application by chiefs and headmen holding junior positions in the colonial administration and exploiting such positions for gaining petty privileges, ensured that it bore little real relationship to the law of the people before conquest.

At the level of the administration of justice, the courts and the whole apparatus of judges and lawyers existed only for the colonists. For the 'natives', the administration of justice was little more than an aspect of 'native policy' and local government. It was the colonial administrator with little legal training, but extensive training in how to attend to 'native affairs', who did justice in terms of the 'native laws'.

In practice, 'native law' for the Mozambicans meant the inhuman and discriminatory pass and tax laws, it meant the barbaric law that imposed forced labour. In respect of labour conditions, the relations between the indigenous employee and the colonial master were governed by the Native Workers Code and the Rural Workers Code, which, in truth, established work regimes not far short of slavery.

In the spheres of civil and criminal law, the political, civil and criminal status attributed to 'natives' ensured that, because of their alleged primitiveness, the statutes, laws and codes applied to the colonists, would not be applied to them. Only a tiny class of persons of indigenous descent were granted a precarious and humiliating assimilation into the status of the colonists.

As for the day-to-day problems that arose among the people, these were resolved according to so-called local uses and customs. Normally the chiefs and headmen acted as faithful servants of colonialism, and ensured that even these uses and customs were filtered and manipulated according to the interests of colonial administration. Favouritism and corruption further weakened this system. Patriotic and independent chiefs were summarily dealt with.

This was a variant of pluralism that did not seriously consider traditional law as a system of law at all, with its own science and its own dynamic of development, but merely as a set of uses and customs which the 'natives' could use to solve their problems at the lower levels of the administration.

In the concrete conditions of our country, the cultural foundation of pluralism was insensitivity rather than sensitivity, while its political basis was despotism rather than democracy. The struggle for independence, for a national culture and for a national legal system therefore inevitably involved a struggle against legal pluralism. The basing of legal rights and duties on colour, origin, life-style or ethnicity was so bound up with the divisiveness and humiliation imposed by colonialism, that legal pluralism came to be identified with colonialism itself and as a barrier to independence and nationhood.

Unity, the Central Theme in the Struggle for National Liberation

The specific features of the colonialism imposed by Portugal (and underdeveloped colonialism, as it has been called) required us to achieve our independence by means of a ten-year armed struggle and military confrontation.

Since Mozambique is a vast country manifesting great ethnic, linguistic, religious and racial complexity, an immense amount of popular mobilization was necessary to bring about the successful outcome of the national liberation struggle. The creation of a broad front, Frelimo, resulted in the question of national unity posing itself as the dominant question in the process of achieving national independence.

An extract from a text by Samora Machel in relation to preparation for the agricultural year in 1971, issued at the height of the armed struggle, illustrates with rare literary beauty and great realism the importance given by the leadership of Frelimo to the theme of unity.

> When I, a Nyanja, am working the soil side by side with a Nguni, my sweat runs down my body as his sweat runs down his body; we each appreciate the effort of the other, we each feel a bond of unity with the other.
>
> When I from the north learn from a comrade from the south to build an orchard, to water tomatoes that will grow red and plump, when I from the

> centre learn from a comrade from the north how to grow mandioca, which I never knew before, I am learning not only about crops but about unity. I am living in a concrete way the unity of my country, and the unity of my class, and the unity of the working people. I am destroying, with each and every one of these comrades, prejudices based on tribe, on religion, on language, I am destroying everything that is secondary and that divides us. With each plant that we grow, with each drop of sweat and ounce of intelligence that we stir into the soil, so we cultivate our unity.[11]

It is this question of national unity which profoundly underlay the whole process of national liberation in Mozambique and constituted in itself a fundamental battlefield, one as important as the confrontation of arms with the occupant army.

Nowhere was this clearer than in relation to the position which women adopted in our society. It was with the launching of armed struggle that Mozambican women had the historic opportunity to emerge as full members of our society, performing the same duties and achieving the same rights as men in the process of the armed struggle.

There were two main reasons for this; first, the vicissitudes of the war itself. To rebuild life after the constant destruction caused by the enemy in the liberated zones, the women had to do more than just sit back and cook for the soldiers: they had to help transport ammunition and food supplies to the battle fronts. They had to treat the wounded, to be school teachers, to take care of the war orphans, to produce food, to enlist in the militia and to mobilize all the people to fight the enemy. But still more than that, as representatives of more than half of the exploited, they came to understand that they had to fight as soldiers, side by side with the men. Thus in 1967, the Women's Detachment of the Frelimo Army was created. Second, in the concrete case of Mozambique, the political issue of the objectives of the war were always clear; Frelimo's watchword was to achieve independence at all costs, as the only way of building a new society free from hunger, disease, illiteracy, and obscurantism; a progressive and just society without the exploitation of man by man.

In this military, political, and social process, Mozambicans realized that women were great fighters, mobilizers and organizers, that women were understanding, generous, selfless and capable. In fact, our armed struggle was our great forum for consciousness raising and for the political education of all the members of our society.

We say today that our legal system is based on the notion of popular justice, since the people participate directly in the administration of justice, jointly with the organs and entities to whom the state attributes a judicial function; but it was in the liberated zones that for the first time since the advent of colonialism the people exercised judicial power, which they did by means of their participation in the Disciplinary Commissions of Frelimo.

These disciplinary organs operated at the grassroots level and resolved matters involving not only the guerrillas but the population at large in the criminal, civil and security spheres. In addition, the disciplinary committees exercised important educational functions, not in relation to abstract questions of doctrine or belief, but in relation to concrete questions about what the objectives of the struggle were, what was meant by unity, and what was involved in the struggle against tribalism, regionalism and racism. Fundamentally they operated on the basis of active involvement of the people, of constant dialogue.

As Jose Moiane, veteran of the national liberation struggle, later Governor of the province of Maputo, said in an interview:

> By means of the activity we developed to resolve concrete cases with the participation of the people, by means of the process of education, of political explanation, of the actual organization of life and society in the liberated zones, people developed a patriotic consciousness and understood the importance of the tasks which each moment of struggle brought their way.
>
> And, of course, later in those zones people began to marry without thinking about tribe; fighters from Maputo and Gaza (in the south) married young girls from Tete and Niassa (in the north) and integrated themselves into the culture of these regions. I, myself, when I operated in Niassa and Tete Provinces felt completely at home. So much so, that I know those provinces better today than I do my own province of origin, which is Gaza. It was the struggle itself that taught us how to take on the dimension of national unity.

Ethnic–Cultural Diversity and Legal Unity

We have tried to show how in a country like Mozambique, instead of being a source of conflict, ethnic–cultural diversity acts as a source for the creation of a national popular culture. We do not ignore the ethnic and cultural particularities of each region of our country, but on the contrary regard them as our riches, as the patrimony of the whole people. Each is a partial aspect of our global culture, of our overall personality as Mozambicans and as men and women of Africa.

The formation of the Mozambican nation as we know it today is the culmination of unification of various kingdoms, of various tribal and ethnic groups, in relation to which the brutal impact of colonialism was only one factor (it was not colonialism that united Mozambique, but a united struggle against colonialism). After independence, this sentiment of national unity has been further challenged and developed. There is cultural interchange between the north, the south and the centre, which constitutes one of the terms of the debate.

In nursery schools and high schools, in cultural and literary associations, in the media, we find expressed the songs, dances, stories and oral tradition of all the zones of our country. The recently held Extraordinary Conference of the

Organization of Mozambican Women, for example, was the culmination of a year long process of research and interaction through the length and breadth of the country, involving meetings, largely in the rural areas, in which perhaps half a million women participated and expressed their opinions of various social and traditional practices, such as initiation rites and marriage settlements. I had the privilege of taking part in this process, both as a woman and as a lawyer.

The extremely rich information which we gathered in villages, schools, hospitals, factories and other productive enterprises, was thereafter subjected to collective scientific analysis (which is not completed yet) by our psychologists, historians, sociologists and lawyers. The study of our social reality is a subject for which our passion continues to grow. We lawyers need increasingly to understand the concrete complexity of our society, since only in this way can we create and apply laws which serve our people and reflect our cultural reality and stage of economic development.

But legal pluralism is not the only way to recognize and express the ethnic–cultural diversity of a country. We do not for a moment suggest that all African countries (in the great majority followers of pluralism) should immediately adopt unitary systems. We just wish to say that as far as we are concerned the creation of a unified legal system was an important step in the guaranteeing of the real equality of all our citizens before the law. The question, therefore, is not whether traditional law should be elevated or subordinated.

Traditional law in Mozambique, as traditional law in all African countries, has a dynamic and vitality of its own. It is not composed of rigid, compartmentalized and impersonal norms. Reflecting its character as part of oral tradition, as part of the symbolical life of the people, of the community life of social interaction and mutual aid, of respect for the ancestors and for the elderly, traditional law is, in addition to being law, part of our culture.

Its dynamic and vital quality is to a great degree infused into our new emerging law. This is explained as follows:

The new Mozambican legal order is made up of three essential components: first, the new laws which clearly reflect the popular nature of our power and the principles which govern the building of a new society; second, norms inherited from the colonial legal regime which are still in force partly because of our inability to undertake the massive legislative reform necessary to transform all areas of our life, partly because they tend to apply to the less crucial areas of our life and are not inconsistent with our Constitution (which in terms of Article 79 automatically revokes all existing legislation not in keeping with the Constitution); third, certain principles, not so much norms as ways of seeing and dealing with problems, which come from traditional law.

Thus the *Courts Act 1978*, provides for the collegiality of judges in all the courts, the active participation of people in trials, decisions based on good sense and justice (at the level of the locality), an attempt always to reconcile the parties, public criticism and performance of community service. All these principles stem from the culture of the people, because traditionally they formed part of the life of the people.

These are positive aspects of traditional law taken over by new generations, not in terms of specific rules of traditional law recognized by the legal order, but as aspects of the cultural life of the people, as parts of our very being, since they express our personality and our very selves, the kind of people we are.

In his well-known study T. O. Elias[2] summarizes principles of traditional law in Africa, which appear as principles of our system of popular justice.

> We should not minimize the advantages which African courts and their procedures may have possessed:
> 1. Justice was popular, in the sense that people understood the mechanisms and objectives of the judicial process and the law applied. The people participated in the courts.
> 2. Justice was local and rapid. The main concern of traditional African courts was to do justice in the local community, rather than to have administrative efficiency or carry out the will of central organs.
> 3. Justice was simple and flexible. There were no elaborate procedural codes or complex forms of proof, although in practice there were certain practical rules in relation to evidence. The judges did not merely carry out the law, above all, they sought solutions for disputes.
> 4. The apparatus for extra-judicial arbitration was always there.

At the same time, while recognizing these considerable virtues, we must not hesitate to turn our backs on and condemn those rules and principles of traditional law which today we consider negative inasmuch as they reflect the class nature of traditional–feudal society, and inasmuch as they were designed to reinforce social and property inequalities between men and women, and between the rulers and the people; that is, inasmuch as they reflected feudal relations of production which belong to the past.

We move away from their application in the day-to-day life of the courts, while recognizing their historical and cultural value as part of our past and recording and preserving them as part of the historic patrimony of the people. The judges are no longer chosen on the basis of lineage or religious office, but are elected by the people. The rules they apply are no longer the superstructural norms of traditional feudal society, but the rules of new codes of behaviour which the people themselves are creating.

What we wish to construct is something new, built by ourselves. We want to grow as people, we want progress, and as such we need to dominate science and technology, and this includes the science of law. Taking our place as an equal in the community of nations in no way inhibits us from feeling ourselves to be a deeply integrated part of our continent, of the African continent. On the contrary, we express our African-ness through transformation and trying to build a new society, and not through trying to mask the difficulties of the present with an idyllic vision of the past.

Index

Abel, Professor Richard, 59
access to law, 10, 46-54
adoption, 19
African justice, 11
Africanization, 1
age of consent, 92
Agro-Industrial Complex of the Limpopo, 34
alcoholism, 60
alienation from legal system, 51
Allott, Professor, 56, 60
Amnesty International, 15
animals, control of hunting of, 10
armed struggle, 4, 30-1, 38, 46, 55, 94, 113; and women, 128
army, transformation of, 13

Babalala, 86
bar, constitution of, 21
beatings of prisoners, 80
Bila, John, 74-85
black market, 14-15, 21, 116-20; in brides, 107
breaking stones, as punishment, 81
bride-price *see lobolo*
British colonialism, 2

Cabral, Rosa, 80
Catholic church, 30, 56, 62
chiefs, system of, 2, 13, 20, 58, 59, 74, 96, 127; destruction of, 24
child marriages, 16-17, 61, 73, 92, 95, 98, 103, 107, 108
children: custody of, 19, 67, 73, 89, 90, 98; interests of, 72; maintenance of, 77, 100, 101
Chile, 115
China, 120
Christian system of marriage, 69, 90
Christianity, 2, 17, 66, 91
cipaios, 82-3
civil marriage, 69-70, 91
co-operatives, 8, 9, 10, 14, 34, 38, 40, 41, 66, 115
colonial legal system, 23, 88, 101, 126-7
Colonial Statute, Portuguese, 84
colonialism, 3, 28-9, 78-85; treatment of servants, 79-81
commercialization of brides, 87, 106
communal villages, 40, 41, 75; family relationships in, 70
community courts, 5 *see also* people's tribunals
Company of Niassa, 29
Company of Zambezia, 29
consciousness: emphasis on, 20; creation of, 44
Constitution of Mozambique, 1, 7, 9, 13, 30, 39, 40, 43, 46, 53, 64, 65, 70, 100, 130
constitution, Salazarist, 84
counter-revolution, 114-15
countryside, socialization of, 8
court structure, 10; development of, 4, 16
Courts Act (1978), 4, 74, 130
crèches, 109
customs and usages, 5

de facto unions, 59, 60, 73, 101, 104, 108, 109; dissolution of, 103; recognition of, 18
debt: family, 90; incurred via *lobolo*, 102
defence, right to, 50-1
denationalization, of land, 39
Disciplinary Commission of Frelimo, 128-9
divorce, 56, 67, 69, 76, 77, 78, 91, 92, 98, 99, 101, 102, 104; types of, 18
drunkenness of husbands, 77, 100
dualist legal system under colonialism, 126-7
dynamizing groups, 99

ecological questions, 10, 33
economic law, 14
Economic Rehabilitation Programme, 15
electoral law, 13
Elias, T.O., 131
elitism of legal systems, 3
equal rights for women, 18
exploitation, abolition of, 114

family, diversity of Mozambican, 66-70
family code, 60
family disputes, 22
family farming, 34, 40
family law, 16-20, 24, 41, 47, 61; transformation of, 64-85
Family Law Project, 43, 101-3
farms: privately-owned, 40; state-owned, 9, 40
fascism, 2, 13, 23, 84, 118
feudalism, 28, 29, 31, 58, 74, 95, 131
fines, 14
First National Conference of Justice, 4
food aid, 8
food, problem of, 115, 116, 117, 120
forced labour, 2, 29, 58, 74, 80-2, 83
Ford Foundation, 25
forests, control of burning of, 10, 42
fraud, 50
Frelimo, 1, 7, 11, 30, 38, 64, 66, 70, 94, 99, 108, 111, 112, 113, 116, 127, 128

gerontocracy, 59
Green Zones, 9, 42

Hambene, Mi, 86
health as hygiene, 113
Hlonipane, 86
hoarding of food, 52
Honwana, Manuel, 87
Honwana, Raul, 86, 91
human rights, 15, 16
Hunguana, Mutxeketxa, 86

illiteracy, of judges, 42, 57, 72, 75, 99
indigenous law, in relation to imposed law, 16, 124
indigenous natives, rights of, 30
informal sector of economy, 14
inheritance, question of, 94, 98
initiation rites, 17, 73, 98
Institute of African Studies, Harvard University, 6
investment, foreign, 9, 14, 41
Islam, 17, 56, 62, 66, 93, 125

Jounod, Henri, 89-91, 95, 109
judges, 42, 43, 46, 47, 57, 72, 76, 87, 99, 119, 120, 126; collegiality of, 130; community, 23; courses for, 54; elected, 24, 75; out of touch, 118; payment of, 11; professional, 23, 24
justice brigades, 4, 55, 66
justice: in locality, 131; speed of, 131

land: abolition of private ownership of, 31; ceases to be commodity, 41; inalienability of, 32; ownership of, by State, 7, 27, 31, 37; ownership of, under colonialism, 38; relations on, 6; right to work, 32; transfer of use by succession, 36
Land Act regulations (1988), 9-10
Land Fund, 32
land law, 27-45
Land Law (1979), 27; programmatic nature of, 42; purposes of, 31
land occupation, 29-30
land titleholders, obligations of, 33
land use, 33, 34, 35; changes of, 8; efficiency of, 43; right to, 40
language of law, to be understandable, 12
languages of Mozambique, 125
Law Faculty: closure of, 14-15, 20, 112; reopened, 15, 21
Law on Judicial Organization (1978), 4
law schools, 3
lawyers, 11, 23, 43, 45, 46, 47, 52, 76, 113, 118, 124, 126, 130; access to, 51; attacks on, 112; departure of, after independence, 51; sent abroad for study, 21; training of, 52
leasehold rights, 41
legal aid, 21, 50-1, 53
legal education, 118
legal systems, informal, 24
legality: revolutionary, 27; socialist, 12, 14, 15, 16, 20, 22, 111-23 (in China, 120; in USSR, 120)
liberated zones, 1, 113
literacy, 11, 12
lobolo, 16-17, 66, 67, 69, 72, 73, 76, 86-109; and liberation of women, 93-7; aspects of, 89-92; forms of, 92; ignored by State, as institution, 98; meaning of, 68; monetary value of, ceiling placed on, 106, 107; national debate on, 62; present status of, 97-100

Machel, Samora, 1, 5, 6, 8, 43, 51, 93-5, 104, 111, 113, 121-2, 127
mahari, 68-9
Malawi, 71
Marks, Shula, 67
marriage, 18, 56, 62, 129; Christian

system of, 69, 90; civil, 69-70, 91; concept of, 87, 99, 102; demonetarization of, 102; matrilineal system of, 66-8; Muslim system of, 18, 68; non-registered, 78; patrilineal system of, 68; public recognition of, 72; registration of, 60, 78, 92, 103; State protection of, 97; traditional, 105
marriage register, creation of, 90
Massangalane, Nwa, 86
Massinga, 86
matrilineal system of marriage, 66-8
matrilineality, 56, 70, 93
matrimonial assets, distribution of, 19
Missionary Accord (1940), 30
Moiane, José, 96, 129
monogamy, 70, 99
morality, of liberation, 113
Moreira da Fonseca, Judge, 78
mortgage, 32, 38
Mozambique, creation of entity, 129
multi-racialism, concept of, 2
murder, 22, 48-50
Muslim judicial structures, 73, 101
Muslim system of marriage, 68

National Institute of Legal Aid, 21
National Land Register, 36
National Parks, 8
nationalization, 51; of education, 31; of land, 39; of medicine, 31
Native Tax, 82
Native Workers Code, 126
Nhaca, Naly, 87
nikah ceremony, 68, 93
Norwegian Agency for Development (NORAD), 25

oral tradition, 130
Organization of Mozambican Women (OMM), 17; conference of, 104-6, 107, 108, 130

palmatoria punishment, 2, 78, 81
paper, shortage of, 12, 20
pass laws, 79, 126
paternalism, 71
patrilineal system of marriage, 68
patrilineality, 56, 67, 92, 93
peasants, 5, 40, 42, 44; African, 8; Portuguese, 8
people's tribunals, 5, 11, 24, 54-63, 87, 99, 101, 102, 123; creation of, 46-54; records of, 76-8
Pereira, Silva, 79
pette, 67
PIDE secret police, 2, 13
pluralism, 19; of legal systems, 57, 83; transcendence of, 124-31
police, 121-2; transformation of, 13
polygamy, 16-17, 56, 61, 68, 69, 73, 76, 77, 90, 92, 94, 95, 98, 100, 103, 104, 107, 108
popular assemblies, creation of, 13
popular justice, 43, 64, 111-23, 131; criteria of, 124; evolution of, 58-60; meaning of, 55; relation to professional, 22
population movements, 30; effects of, 8
Portugal, 23, 39, 84, 96, 118, 125, 127
Portuguese colonialism, 1-4, 28-30, 58, 86, 92, 119, 125, 126
Portuguese language not understood, 12
Portuguese legal system, 54, 61, 74-85, 99, 103 *see also* colonial legal system
prazeiros, 29
prazos, 29, 34, 36
prices, deregulation of, 21
prison, 2, 22, 33, 52, 80; transformation of, 13
prisoners, 20: assaults on, 121; overcrowding of, 22
private legal practice, abolition of, 12, 51
property: categories of, 7-8, 41; division of, 100; private, non-recognition of, 41; transmission of, 67
property law, changed nature of, 41
protected zones, 35
protracted struggle, concept of, 71
public defenders, 52-3
publication of laws, 12-13, 20, 28

racism, struggle against, 52
rape, 22
reconciliation, as aim of law, 130
regionalism, struggle against, 19, 52
rent, 32, 38
reserves, land, 35
responsibles, 77, 78
revolution, 114-15
Rhodesia, 114
royal companies, 29
Rural Workers Code, 126

Sachs, Albie, 3
Salazar, Dr Antonio, 84
scholars, role of, 44
secret ballots, 14
servants, under colonialism, 79-81
Service Books, 79
sexism, 59
slavery, 39

socialism, 16, 21, 24, 31, 34; African, concept of, 1-2
South Africa, 2, 12, 39, 114
State Procurator, office of, 46
subsistence farming, 39
suffrage, exclusion of persons from, 13
Supreme Court, 4

Tanzania, 71
taxation, 2, 126
taxes: collection of, 58, 74, 96; exemption from, 83; non-payment of, 82
Third World romanticism, 6
torture, 113
traditional law, 44, 49, 60, 61, 64, 88, 101, 130; abolition of, 74; concept of, 65; principles of, 131; significance of, 75-6
transport sector, pirate, 21
transport to court, 20, 48
tribal systems, 56
tribalism, struggle against, 5, 6, 19, 52
triumphalism, 6
Tsonga people, 89

Union of Soviet Socialist Republics (USSR), 120
unitary legal system: possibility of, 70-6; problem of, 60-3
unity: as theme of national liberation, 127-9; legal, 129-31

Vatican, 30
Vilanculo, Nwa, 86
Vulande, 86

war, effects of, 8, 20 (on role of women, 20, 95)
Welch, Gita, 3, 87
whipping as punishment, 14, 20, 112, 114, 117, 119
widows, inheritance of, 89, 90, 108
wife beating, 60
witches, burning of, 48-9
wives, second, 77
women, 55, 56, 59, 120, 128; and armed struggle, 128; as workers, 9; effects of war on, 20, 95; liberation of, 65, 86-109
women and men, relations between, 65, 72, 94-5, 97, 131
Women's Detachment of Liberation Army, 95, 128
Women's Movement, 42, 47, 66, 73, 74, 99
Women's Organization, 62
women's rights, 17, 20, 63, 76, 97

young people, role of, 59
youth Movement, 66, 74